BECOMING STRONG

Impoverished Women and the Struggle to Overcome Violence

"My future looks good at this present time in my life." A surprising statement, perhaps, coming from a 36-year-old homeless woman, but this quote is typical of the majority of women to whom the reader will be introduced in this book.

Becoming Strong: Impoverished Women and the Struggle to Overcome Violence offers a radical departure from the orthodox view of homeless women as weak, lacking in agency, and/or pathological. Drawing on research conducted with homeless women in three U.S. cities (Los Angeles, Chicago, and Detroit), authors Laura Huey and Ryan Broll present an alternative view that is rooted primarily in the thoughts, beliefs, and experiences of homeless women themselves. Through analysis of nearly 200 semi-structured interviews with homeless women, it is revealed that there is no singular response to the various types of trauma these women have experienced – from violent victimization to sudden deaths of loved ones to the process of becoming homeless itself. Instead, the women interviewed exhibited a broad range of responses, which included both symptoms of trauma and signs of resiliency. And, rather than being passive victims of circumstance, most of the women see themselves as strong individuals, oriented towards the future and determined to build something better for their lives.

Being Strong not only examines trauma and the role it can play in shaping homeless women's lives, but also explores how women can and do grow from traumatic experiences. It also looks at those situations where women remain trapped in negative patterns and offers solutions for responding to issues that perpetuate the cycle of female homelessness. In presenting its findings, this book draws upon current research and theories from diverse fields within sociology, criminology, and psychology, offering readers a complex view of a set of complex issues.

LAURA HUEY is a professor in the Department of Sociology at the University of Western Ontario.

RYAN BROLL is an assistant professor in the Department of Sociology and Anthropology at the University of Guelph.

LAURA HUEY AND RYAN BROLL

Becoming Strong

Impoverished Women and the Struggle to Overcome Violence

UNIVERSITY OF TORONTO PRESS
Toronto Buffalo London

ISBN 978-1-4426-4950-7 (cloth)
ISBN 978-1-4426-2685-0 (paper)

Library and Archives Canada Cataloguing in Publication

Huey, Laura, author
Becoming strong : impoverished women and the struggle
to overcome violence / Laura Huey and Ryan Broll.

Includes bibliographical references and index.
Issued in print and electronic formats.
ISBN 978-1-4426-4950-7 (cloth)
ISBN 978-1-4426-2685-0 (pbk.)

1. Homeless women – Violence against – United States. 2. Homeless
women – United States – Social conditions. 3. Violence – Psychological
aspects. I. Broll, Ryan, 1966–, author II. Title.

HV4505.H84 2018   305.48'442   C2017-907845-3

The authors acknowledge the assistance of the
J.B. Smallman Publication Fund, and the Faculty of Social Science,
the University of Western Ontario.

University of Toronto Press acknowledges the financial assistance to its
publishing program of the Canada Council for the Arts and the Ontario Arts
Council, an agency of the Government of Ontario.

 Canada Council Conseil des Arts
for the Arts du Canada

 ONTARIO ARTS COUNCIL
CONSEIL DES ARTS DE L'ONTARIO
an Ontario government agency
un organisme du gouvernement de l'Ontario

Funded by the   Financé par le
Government   gouvernement
of Canada   du Canada  Canadä

Contents

Tables and Photographs

Tables

Photographs

BECOMING STRONG

Impoverished Women and the Struggle to Overcome Violence

Introduction

This book is intended to offer a view into the struggles of those homeless women who have been exposed to violence and are attempting to overcome its effects, while simultaneously coping with many other forms of adversity. Drawing on interviews conducted with women in Chicago, Detroit, and Los Angeles, we illuminate aspects of their individual journeys, and provide portraits of these women that are rooted primarily in their thoughts, beliefs, and experiences as they attempt the process of becoming resilient, with some even successfully achieving this state. What these interviews reveal is that there is no singular response to violent victimization. Instead, the women encountered exhibited a broad range of responses. One thing that most did share, however, was that they saw themselves as "survivors" who were at various stages in the process of overcoming violence. Their words reveal that where they see themselves in that process is largely influenced by a set of both internal and external factors – from their own personality traits to their ability to draw support from their social networks.

In the pages that follow, we also draw widely on the relevant research on victimization, trauma, and resilience from the fields of sociology, criminology, psychology, and social work. The research literature provides a context for understanding the violence that impoverished women face, as well as its mental and emotional effects. However, trauma is only half of the equation. We also rely on a body of research that examines the impact of resilience determinants (personal traits and interpersonal factors) and resilience processes (coping strategies) on trauma survivors in order to enhance our understanding of how women, who typically have the fewest possible resources upon which to draw, attempt to access their own personal strengths and develop the coping skills to move past violence. In essence, it is the central goal of this book to pair women's stories with what is known about trauma and resilience to help us better identify women's strengths and build upon them in order to ease their transition into recovery.

Violence

Research has consistently shown that homeless women are more likely to be physically and sexually assaulted than domiciled women, even when controlling for socio-economic status (Perron et al. 2008). In one study, almost one-quarter of homeless women had been physically or sexually assaulted in the last thirty days alone (Wenzel, Koegel, and Gelberg 2000). Other researchers have demonstrated that women become more vulnerable to violent victimization when they become homeless (D'Ercole and Struening 1990; Evans and Forsyth 2004; Wenzel, Koegel, and Gelberg 2000; Wenzel, Leake, and Gelberg 2001). This is not particularly surprising: homeless women are often forced by circumstance to participate in subsistence activities that increase their risk of victimization (Wesely and Wright 2009). The risk of victimization on the streets is even higher for those with a history of serious mental illness (Goodman, Dutton, and Harris 1997; Larney et al. 2009).

Even before they become homeless, many homeless women have extensive histories of violent victimization. In fact, as will be further discussed in the next chapter, violence is considered a leading pathway into homelessness for some women. Several studies have demonstrated that homeless women are victimized frequently, often beginning early in their lives (Bassuk, Perloff, and Dawson 2001; Bassuk et al. 2010; D'Ercole and Struening 1990). D'Ercole and Struening (1990) found that 23 per cent of the female shelter users they interviewed in New York City reported childhood sexual abuse. North and Smith (1992) studied homeless women in St. Louis and similarly reported that 23 per cent of the women they interviewed had been sexually abused in childhood. Some have suggested that these studies likely underestimate the actual rate of childhood sexual abuse among homeless women,[1] meaning that

---

1 This critique relates to the methodology of both studies. D'Ercole and Struening (1990) focused on molestation, a rather narrow definition of childhood sexual abuse, whereas North and Smith (1992) did not clearly provide examples of abuse to their participants.

true rates of abuse might be considerably higher. Indeed, in a study of 974 homeless women in Los Angeles, Wenzel, Andersen, Gifford, and Gelberg (2001) found that 32 per cent had been sexually abused in childhood. Sadly, abuse within homeless women's families of origin is often so common that they consider it normal, and it is sometimes only after years of intense counselling that women realize violence should not have been part of their childhoods (Anderson and Imle 2001).

Violent victimization is associated with many adverse social and emotional outcomes (Hudson et al. 2010). Furthermore, victimization has been found to account for a significant amount of variation in homeless women's emotional distress (Goodman et al. 1997). The effects of that distress on homeless women is well understood within the research literature (Lam and Rosenheck 1998; Perron et al. 2008; Tsai et al. 2015). What is less well understood is both the extent to which some of these same women "move past" the effects of violence and other traumatic episodes, and the processes they undergo in their quest to become resilient.

Resilience (in Its Many Forms)

Within the social scientific literature, resilience is understood as a "combination of innate personality traits and environmental influences that serve to protect individuals from the harmful psychological effects of trauma or severe stress, enabling them to lead satisfying and productive lives" (Bogar and Hulse-Killacky 2006, 319). Or, more simply, as "the capacity to do well despite adverse experience" (Gilligan 2000, 37). While research into the social/structural and personal factors influencing resilience development has grown in relation to various segments of the population, with the exception of a growing literature on homeless youth and coping (Karabanow and Kidd 2014; Perron, Cleverley, and Kidd 2014; Ferguson, Bender, and Thompson 2015), little research has examined the capacity for resilience among homeless adults.[2] This is particularly the case for homeless women, who, as we have seen, represent a segment of the population that experiences disproportionate levels of violence (Wesely and Wright 2009).

In this book, we use several key concepts from the resilience literature as an explanatory framework for understanding how homeless women

---

2 See Stump and Smith (2008), Huey, Fthenos, and Hryniewicz (2012), and Bonugli, Lesser, and Escandon (2013), for three notable exceptions.

not only cope with both homelessness and the after-effects of violence but also enter and move through the process of becoming resilient. We also draw on this literature to explore those instances in which women remain "stuck" and unable to move forward emotionally, mentally, physically, or otherwise from where they are currently situated. Most importantly, we employ the concept of "hidden resilience" (Ungar 2004, 2005, 2006) to argue that conventional standards of evaluating or conceptualizing "resilience" are not sufficiently sensitive to the conditions within which such women exist and, particularly, to the frequent lack of alternate coping mechanisms or therapeutic alternatives for these individuals. To help the reader navigate the ideas presented in this book, we next present the definitions for the key concepts that appear in the pages that follow.

Trauma

Central to any discussion of resilience is the concept of trauma, particularly, its relationship to violence. Trauma in this context is perhaps best defined as an emotional, mental, or physiological set of responses to a significant life event (CAMH 2016), a life event so shattering for the individual that it violates "foundations of trust." This trust might have been previously anchored in relations between individuals, tied to one's own self, or embedded in one's sense of security in her environment or her place in the world. The results of such losses are "feelings of helplessness, pain, and confusion" (Bonugli, Lesser, and Escandon 2013, 833). The experience of interpersonal violence, whether as victim or witness, is a traumatic experience for most people. This is not simply our conjecture; a wealth of research, including several systematic reviews and meta-analyses, has demonstrated that violent victimization has significant mental and emotional impacts on individuals (Tsai et al. 2015). Among those effects are depression, anxiety, hyperarousal, social isolation, marital problems, emotional reactivity, and the worsening of pre-existing mental health issues (Collishaw et al. 2007; Cinamon, Muller, and Rosenkranz 2014). We also know that repeat victimization (or "polyvictimization"), as well as the addition of other adverse conditions (such as homelessness), can increase the risk of poor physical, mental, and social outcomes (Hamilton, Poza, and Washington 2011). As Cinamon, Muller, and Rosenkranz (2014, 725) summarize the relevant literature, "the detrimental effects of interpersonal violence and childhood trauma on later functioning are well known."

Resilience

As some scholars have remarked, the construct of resilience is a bit ambiguous (Waaktaar and Torgersen 2010). There are many conceptions as to what constitutes resilience, and increasingly so as researchers have begun to recognize that the process of overcoming trauma – and what that might look like for specific individuals and groups – is context-dependent (Ungar 2006; S. Thompson et al. 2013). A frequently cited definition of resilience is "the process of, capacity for, or outcome of successful adaptation despite challenging or threatening circumstances" (Masten, Best, and Garmezy 1990, 426). With respect to the experience of violent victimization, some have suggested it is the ability of individuals to "recover," "move on from," "achieve closure on," or "overcome" the event and any negative after-effects (Canvin et al. 2009; Huey, Fthenos, and Hryniewicz 2012). The definition we employ in this book is drawn from Coulter (2014, 50): "the ability to resist, cope with or recover from serious physical and psychological difficulties."

Borrowing from the emergent literature on resilience within homeless populations, we might also say – in the case of homeless women – that resilience is also the ability to adapt to one's environment and successfully function within that environment to meet individual needs and personal goals (S. Thompson et al. 2013). The ability to adapt to this unique and challenging environment is what Ungar (2004, 2006) has termed "hidden resilience." In the context of discussing the development of "street smarts" by homeless youth, Sanna Thompson et al. (2013, 60) highlight the operation of hidden resilience when they observe that while homeless youth who exercise street smarts might not be engaging in "'prosocial' behaviours in a traditional sense, these young people are developing competencies unique to their environment that assist them in enduring their daily existence."

One aspect of the resilience literature with which there is common agreement, and is necessary to flag in advance of our larger discussion in chapter 3, is that achieving resilience is typically a dynamic and fluid process rather than a linear trajectory (Tusaie and Dyer 2004; Canvin et al. 2009). Individuals move forward, or not, at their own individual pace, and many face obstacles and setbacks along the way (Canvin et al. 2009; Huey, Fthenos, and Hryniewicz 2012; Meichenbaum 2013). In this book, we borrow from women's own terminology and employ the term "stuck" to describe when individuals feel blocked – whether emotionally, mentally, physically, or otherwise – from moving forward. The extent to which an individual can "move on" or remain "stuck" is best described as a complex, interactional process involving both internal and external supports (Werner and Smith 2001).

Resilience Determinants

Much of the literature explains individual transitions through the resilience process as a product of the interactions between two phenomena: risk and protective factors (Rutter 1987). Previous research on homelessness has amply demonstrated that being either unhoused or precariously housed is a significant risk factor (Masten et al. 2014; Ferguson, Bender, and Thompson 2015), and this is also evident throughout the material presented in this book. What *we* highlight are those protective factors that help women become resilient. Among protective factors, we include various personal qualities and social relationships that are frequently referred to by researchers as "resilience determinants." These are factors known to be associated with increased ability to successfully overcome trauma and other adverse conditions (Bogar and Hulse-Killacky 2006). Although the term "determinant" might suggest otherwise, we do caution that whereas these factors are clearly associated with increased resilience, they are not "magic bullets" (Meichenbaum 2013, 326).

For personal qualities, we could point to self-efficacy, adaptability, being action-oriented, personal mastery, social competency, and problem-solving skills as frequently cited protective factors (Benard 1991; Connor and Davidson 2003; Bender et al. 2007; Kidd and Davidson 2007). Also commonly noted is the importance of social and spiritual supports, or determinants, such as strong family ties, a caring partner, or a religious community (Smith et al. 2011; McClendon and Lane 2014). It is the ability of individuals to draw on these internal and external supports that aids them in developing resilience. As Cyrulnik (2009, 51) has said of the operation of these two sets of factors: "resilience is a mesh, not a substance. We are forced to knit ourselves, using the people and things we meet in our emotional and social environments."

Coping

Resilience determinants are only one part of the overall picture. Coping – that is the techniques or strategies individuals use to deal with violence and its after-effects – is another important factor. The literature frequently divides coping into two types: adaptive or pro-social ("healthy" forms) and maladaptive or avoidant ("unhealthy" forms) (Seiffge-Krenke 2004). The former may include seeking support from peers, using positive support systems, engaging in community activities, helping others, exercising, or taking positive steps to change one's life (Baker and Berenbaum 2007; Diaz and Motta 2008; Bender et al. 2007). The latter are typically described as including alcohol or drug abuse, excessive sleeping, social withdrawal and emotion or problem avoidance (Kidd and Davidson 2007; Ferguson, Bender, and Thompson 2015).

While it is the case that some negative coping strategies – such as alcohol or substance abuse – cannot be easily, if ever, understood as useful strategies for fostering resilience, it is important to remember that others might be when individual circumstances are considered. For example, social withdrawal within one setting might appear to be an avoidant, and thus maladaptive, coping strategy, but, within the space of the streets, it can be a viable strategy of self-protection. For this reason, unless one of our interviewees spoke directly about how the coping strategies they employed were harming them or were counter-productive to their goals, we generally avoid making attributions as to whether an activity or pursuit was negative or positive for the woman involved. For us, coping is simply an attempt by an individual to respond to traumatic experiences and other stressors using strategies aimed at overcoming those experiences and/or minimizing their adverse effects.

The Data

To explore the process by which homeless female victims of violence develop resilience, we extracted the results of 187 of 282 in-depth qualitative interviews from two larger studies conducted from June 2011 to May 2014 in three American cities purposively selected because they are major metropolitan centres with substantial homeless populations: Detroit, Chicago, and Los Angeles. These interviews were selected because they met two key criteria: (1) the participant had been a victim of violence and had discussed her experiences with the interviewer, and (2) she had also answered questions on resilience and where she saw herself in the process of becoming resilient. Interview data from study participants who had not been victims of violence were excluded; we also excluded partial or incomplete interviews ($n = 95$).

To provide a more complete understanding of where our data come from, we offer a brief introduction to the two larger studies. The first project, which ran from 2011 to 2012, explored issues related to access to services by homeless women who had been victims of violence. To locate potential research participants, we developed a non-probability sample consisting of the maximum number of service agencies working with homeless women in Detroit and Chicago, and asked each organization if they would agree to facilitate our research. Facilitation was defined as providing access to organizational space, staff, and clients. In total, thirteen shelters agreed to participate. Once the team arrived, we would explain our project and individual participants would self-select – that is, participants chose to be interviewed after hearing we were conducting a study on criminal victimization and access to services post-victimization.

Our eligibility requirements – aside from willingness to participate – were a minimum age of eighteen, current homelessness, and evidence of a clear capacity to understand the nature of consent. For each participant, we explained the nature of the study, reviewed the informed consent forms, and outlined the types of questions we would be asking. Once we were assured that they understood the nature of their participation and had signed the consent form, we began the interview. Interviews were typically of an hour's duration and each was recorded with the knowledge and consent of the participant.

The first preliminary interviews were conducted using a basic interview guide covering six key areas: (1) basic demographic information; (2) experiences of victimization over the life course; (3) physical, emotional, and mental effects of victimization; (4) experiences of accessing healthcare providers post-victimization; (5) willingness to use healthcare services (physician, hospitals, mental health counsellors); and (6) facilitators and barriers to accessing health services post-victimization. After these exploratory interviews were analysed, we realized that, unprompted, women were also talking about something we hadn't previously thought to ask about: their experiences in relation to the resilience process. Intrigued by what they were telling us, the interview guide was amended to include a series of questions concerning resilience and coping factors, as well as how participants self-identified in terms of "strong" versus "weak" or "vulnerable," or "moving on" versus "being stuck." These terms were selected because they were the ones women used most frequently to self-describe their own attitudes and behaviours in discussions of coping and resilience.

The second study in Los Angeles was directly shaped by what we learned in Detroit and Chicago. While more broadly focused on the range of trauma impoverished women typically experience beyond violence, this study was also more narrowly focused on the resilience process. This project, which ran from August 2013 to May 2014, thus included questions specifically intended to explore "resilience determinants" (aspects of one's personality) and "resilience processes" (coping strategies employed), two key concepts that had emerged in our earlier work in Chicago and Detroit.

As we had done in Chicago and Detroit, we began by developing a non-probability sample of the maximum number of shelters and transitional housing programs that work with homeless women in Los Angeles County. A team member then contacted each of these programs to see if they would agree to participate in the study by facilitating access to their clients. In total, eight agencies agreed. Across the two studies in Detroit, Chicago, and Los Angeles County, approximately 50 per cent of eligible shelters agreed to participate. As was the case in our earlier work, all individuals who agreed to be interviewed at participating sites self-selected after hearing about the goals of our study. To be included as a participant, the potential interviewee had to be a minimum of eighteen years of age, using shelter services, and able to provide informed consent. On average, interviews were typically forty minutes in duration and were conducted using an interview guide.

Each team member received pre-field training in qualitative interviewing techniques and, under the guidance of two experienced team members, received further training and supervision in the field on techniques and use of the interview guide. The interview guide consisted of questions related to six key areas: (1) basic demographic information; (2) traumatic events over the life course; (3) participant self-identification in relation to the resilience process; (4) resilience determinants (personality characteristics); (5) resilience processes (coping skills); and (6) suggestions for services.

Data were analysed using theoretical thematic analysis, a flexible and iterative approach to analysing data derived from in-depth qualitative interviews (Braun and Clarke 2006). Our intention was to identify those resilience determinants and coping strategies used by homeless women to manage experiences of violent victimization. We have included some descriptive statistics derived from participants' interview responses to provide an overview of the participants' demographic characteristics and victimization experiences. Our sample was not selected randomly, and we did not analyse these data using multivariate or inferential techniques, nor was it our intention to do so. Therefore, generalizations beyond the present sample cannot be made.

A Map

The structure of this book is as follows. In chapter 1, we introduce readers to the women who participated in this study, first through an overview of demographic factors, then by examining how women saw themselves in relation to the resilience process.

The focus of chapter 2 is women's experiences with violence in childhood and adulthood, including sexual and physical assault, intimate partner violence (IPV), gang-related violence, and the witnessing of severe violence. What homeless women need to do to survive often increases their risk of victimization; indeed, many women have been extensively victimized before becoming homeless.

Chapter 3 explores the emotional and psychological impacts of violence. Learning more about the life histories of the women interviewed reveals a manifold set of emotional, mental, and other after-effects of violent victimization. Some women experienced intense shame and guilt, blaming themselves for allowing themselves to be victims. Others attributed alcohol and drug dependency to their victimization. Some developed classic symptoms of trauma, particularly signs of anxiety and depression, which they related to their experience of violence (Huey 2016). Others were under psychiatric or other medical treatment, having been diagnosed with these and other trauma-related disorders (notably post-traumatic stress disorder) (Huey and Ricciardelli 2016).

In chapter 4 we explore the resilience process and where women situated themselves in relation to that process. Many felt they had begun the journey and were on their way to achieving a better future. Others felt they had overcome violence and other traumatic experiences, but were still struggling with aspects of the present, principally in the form of ongoing homelessness. Still others felt they were "stuck," not only unable to overcome current obstacles but also to even begin the process of dealing with the experiences of violence.

How do homeless women who have, in some instances, experienced lifetimes of abuse and violence develop resilience? In chapter 5, we shift our focus to what women had to say about "resilience determinants" – that is, whether they attributed their strengths to innate personality traits, learned self-knowledge and skills, spirituality, or networks of social support. Just as not all women self-identify as resilient, not all women found the characteristics or supports necessary to thrive; therefore, we also highlight the circumstances of those women who describe themselves as "weak" as a point of contrast to those who are resilient.

The next chapter concerns the specific strategies the women consciously adopt to deal with past events and/or present adversities. These coping strategies range from mental techniques (such as meditation or the use of positive affirmations) to engaging in forms of creative self-expression (such as painting, music, and bead work) to planning and actualizing future goals (such as school, employment, and family unification). Within chapter 6, we draw on the women's own views of the benefits of these techniques to show how they foster coping.

Chapter 7 begins with a summary of the preceding chapters. This summary allows us to develop a set of key recommendations for helping women move forward based on our findings. In essence, we argue that if so many disadvantaged women can face unimaginable violence and trauma and still try to move forward in their recovery, even more could be accomplished if only they received housing, psychological and other forms of support sensitive to both their strengths and current place on the road to recovery.

Chapter One

The Women

I taught myself … it's real bad, but I taught myself to be more hard to my feelings. A lot of stuff, I can't cry that easy no more. My sister passed … it sounds bad, but … I felt real bad, but I couldn't cry. I compressed my whole feelings, because I was getting hurt just that much. I became numbed. I don't even laugh at different things. It kinda bothers me, though. I don't laugh and I don't cry.

– Tonya

For the past several months, Tonya, a mother of four, has been sleeping with her children on the floors of various church basements in Detroit. Tonya and her children became homeless when her current husband moved to Tennessee and she refused to join him. The reasons for her decision to remain in Detroit become manifestly clear over the course of the interview, as do the factors that gave rise to Tonya having learned to become "hard to [her] feelings."

Tonya traces the development of her emotional shell to a childhood incident. Around the age of eleven, a favourite uncle molested Tonya. The first time it happened, her parents, who were themselves physically abusive towards their children, were downstairs. Tonya fought him off, yelling and cursing loudly, until her mother called her downstairs. Tonya believed that her mother had heard what was going on and knew what her uncle had done, and thus Tonya "hated her after that."

While still a teenager, Tonya married a man she describes as "very violent." His physical assaults and emotional abuse continued long after Tonya had filed for divorce. Sometimes he would break into her new home in the middle of the night and she would find herself being woken up by "getting pulled off the couch by my feet, my head hitting the wall or the floor." The next day he would return to see his children, acting as though nothing had happened. The situation came to a final, violent end three years after Tonya had ended her marriage.

One day he came up to me and my boyfriend and he was like, "I'm going to kill all of y'all. I have 6 bullets." That was exactly what he was saying to us because he seen us at the store. I'm going to kill all 3 kids, which was his kids. "I'm going to kill you, him, then I'mma kill myself that way I won't be in trouble." I'm like, "He crazy." So, we brushed it off. He seen us again. He repeated the same thing. So, I'm like wait a minute, he's saying the same thing, so I need to go and get a gun to protect me and my home. A 12 gauge [shotgun]. I went and got a 12 gauge. I went and took it to the police station and got it registered. We in the house one day ... he keep threatening us ... he climbed through the window with a gun. The kids jumped out the window. My sister ran next door. He came in and he pulled the gun on us. The 12 gauge was in the corner. So, my boyfriend grabbed the 12 gauge. He had it down. Everything happened so fast. All I remember is that I'm too busy calling the police ... my boyfriend shot him and he died right there.

Following her ex-husband's death, Tonya married the boyfriend who had shot and killed him. Tonya's second marriage had its own problems characterized by violence and her new husband's alcoholism. When the issue of sexual assault is raised, Tonya reveals that she has been repeatedly sexually assaulted by her second husband: "Yes, that happened by my own husband ... If we get into a fight, some men feel like sex supposed to make it up. If you don't want to, they will hold you down and do it."

Given everything Tonya has experienced over the course of her life thus far, it is of little surprise to discover that she lives with chronic anxiety and depression, both of which she directly attributes to her experiences with violence. The anxiety has begun to manifest in panic attacks. Bouts of depression have led to suicidal thoughts. "God forgive me, but I thought maybe if I just get rid of me and the kids, maybe we won't have to go through this crap." Shortly after the shooting, she began to put her suicidal thoughts into motion: "I actually called my sister and said, 'Would you keep the kids because I'm thinking about killing myself?'" What pulled Tonya through was her children and the belief she had to live for them.

In the face of everything she has been through, and her continuing struggle to overcome the effects of a lifetime of significant violence, Tonya doesn't hesitate when asked if she sees herself as a strong individual: "I'm overstrong." Tonya has had to become "hard" and "numb" to survive, as she explains it, because, aside from her one sister, she has received little emotional support from her family, and no outside assistance from mental health or other social services to help her cope with the aftermath of violence. Tonya is clear that she does not want to continue struggling with the past; rather, she wants to attend counselling or any other type of program that can help her to begin the process of healing her mental and emotional scars: "I want that opening. I want to be open again, [to] trust a little more." She has not, however, lost her ability to try to draw positive life lessons from her own terrible experiences: "All the stuff that happened to you, helps you in your life … because certain things happened to me, it makes me watch out for my kids on that route."

Within this chapter, we provide some insights into the nature of the sample of women interviewed for this study. We do this by, first, presenting a brief discussion of some relevant demographic factors. We then turn to the issue of homelessness and how various individuals first entered into this state, before looking at the cyclical nature of some of the women's experiences with homelessness. The discussion then moves to an overview of their experiences of violence, followed by an exploration of the extent to which the women who participated self-identify as "strong" or "moving forward," or, conversely, as "weak" and/or "stuck" in relation to both past traumas and present adversity. Through reintroducing the concept of "hidden resilience," we also consider what these self-descriptions might mean in light of what the literature on resilience and coping tells us about these processes.

Demographics

Demographic information was recorded for each interviewee (see Table 1.1). To capture this information, questions were asked about how individuals self-identify with respect to their race and/or ethnicity, their present age, and their length of current homelessness.

Most women interviewed were African American. The next most common racial group represented in our study were White/Caucasian women, who accounted for 18 per cent of our sample. Hispanic/Latina women accounted for 12 per cent of our sample, Native American women for 1 per cent, and Southeast Asian women for 1 per cent.

Table 1.1. Participants' race/ethnicity

Race/ethnicity	N
African American	122
White/Caucasian	34
Hispanic/Latina	23
Biracial	4
Native American	2
Southeast Asian	2
Total	187

About 2 per cent of our sample was comprised of women who identified as biracial.

Issues of race and ethnicity were raised during several of the interviews, with researchers[1] asking specifically about these factors in relation to women's experiences with poverty and violence, their ability to access resources, and/or through discussions of cultural norms regarding speaking about violence outside the home or of seeking help from external sources. With few exceptions, our attempts to focus women's issues on the question of race were rejected by participants. Meda, a thirty-four-year-old African American woman residing in Chicago, was quick to respond to one such attempt: "It's not about the colour. I hate when people do that, when they colourize situations." One of the few exceptions was Becky, a thirty-three-year-old woman who self-described as "Eskimo, Native Alaskan." Becky was simultaneously fighting the Social Security Administration over withdrawal of her benefits, a social service agency over the return of her children, and the police for failing to arrest the man who had recently raped her.[2] When asked later in the interview if she had been able to let go of any of her anger and resentment over things that had haunted her in the past, Becky acknowledged that she still had "a lot to work on," including her feelings about what she considered an inherently racist and classist social system. Sharleen, a fifty-six-year-old African American woman, was another exception. She spoke to the issue of racial oppression when asked about how she dealt with the violence she has seen in the streets: "It didn't really impact me because I come from Texas. I witness white

---

1 Research teams were ethnically diverse and multiracial.
2 Because she had been "drugged and passed out" and was therefore unable to remember clearly what had happened, the police stated they were unable to press charges against Becky's assailant.

Table 1.2. Participants' ages

Age (in years)	N
18–24	24
25–34	23
35–44	35
45–54	68
55–64	31
65+	3
Did not answer	3
Total	187

people burning black people, beating black people. I witness all that. So, I'm used to seeing blood and violence."

The minimum age for inclusion was eighteen. Thus, the youngest participants were eighteen; the oldest was seventy (see Table 1.2). The majority of women interviewed were between the ages of forty-five and sixty-four. Several of the women had become homeless for the first time in their fifties or sixties, whereas others had cycled in and out of homelessness for several decades. One commonality among women in this group was a sense of how difficult it was to be homeless as an older adult. As one sixty-year-old Chicago woman explained, "It's so hard to find work at this age, even if you're qualified."

A number of women fell within the age group of thirty-five to forty-four. These women were also characterized by a diversity of life experiences and reasons for becoming homeless. They were also of various levels of emotional maturity, insight, and wisdom. For example, one thirty-nine-year-old woman in Chicago showed remarkable clarity about her own level of emotional maturity when she said of herself, "I always hung with kids younger than me. Never my age or older. I had the mind set of someone younger. I am just starting to grow up now, but I still act like a kid some days."

One of our smallest age groupings included those aged eighteen to twenty-four. This is not altogether surprising since there are many agencies that provide shelter and other services specifically for young people (i.e., those aged twenty-five and under). Although one of the facilities where we conducted interviews was specifically for younger women, most were either for adult women or mixed-gender adult populations. Of the younger women interviewed, most had recently become homeless after leaving home because of family conflicts, although several advised they had spent years living in institutions or on the streets.

Table 1.3. Length of current homelessness

Length of homelessness	N
1 day–1 year	81
1 year–3 years	56
3 years–10 years	28
More than 10 years	14
Did not answer	8
Total	187

Of the latter group of women, Mariah had been in and out of residential facilities throughout her teenage years. Pregnant at the time of the interview, Mariah had been living with a cousin but became homeless when her cousin was evicted from her apartment. When asked for her age, Mariah replied, "Nineteen. I'm a baby having a baby."

Among women aged twenty-four to thirty-five, some were experiencing their first episode of homelessness, whereas others had been on the streets before or had been involved in aspects of "street life." Toya, thirty-four, had been homeless for the better part of six years. She had been living off and on with family members; however, following the deaths of her mother and grandmother, she struggled to stay housed. As a teenager, she had run with gang members, describing this period of her life as "in the streets running around."

Lastly, three participants chose not to provide their ages. What makes their decision particularly interesting is that each was otherwise forthcoming when discussing other details about her personal life and present situation.

As suggested above, participants had a diverse range of experiences of homelessness. Since many of the women had experienced multiple episodes of homelessness, the first question we asked was about the length of their *current* period of homelessness (see Table 1.3). One woman interviewed had been homeless for only a day, whereas another had spent the better part of twenty years living on the streets and in shelters. Most frequently, the women in our sample had been homeless for a period of less than a year. One woman in this group, Anisha, a twenty-four-year-old Detroit resident, described a common pattern among many women interviewed: she frequently moved between friends' couches, hotels, shelters, and other facilities in order to get help and keep a roof over her head. Describing this process, Anisha said,

It started in January ... I was staying at a friend's house for like two months and that was horrible. Then I went into MATTS[3] and I was there for three weeks. Then I went to McCrest for like two days. I absolutely hated it. Then I stayed at hotel to hotel, whatever I could afford. Then I went into rehab for a month. Now that I've got out, I was staying at a three-quarter[4] house.

During the five weeks prior to the interview, Anisha had been staying at her sixth temporary abode within six months – the Detroit shelter where she was interviewed.

Whereas women who had been homeless for less than one year could often pinpoint an exact date or month in which they had become homeless, women who had been homeless for a period of one to three years were often unable to be exact, offering instead rough estimates. "I've been homeless ... really, like two, three years," Zoila, a thirty-nine-year-old Latina mother, replied to this question. Livvy, a twenty-one-year-old Detroit woman was similarly unsure: "I'd say for about two years."

Our next group was comprised of women who had been homeless for a period of three to ten years. They, too, often had difficulty calculating the length of their current experience of homelessness, frequently because it was punctuated with only brief periods of stable housing. Meda's answer demonstrates this uncertainty: "I've been homeless ... really, like two, three years. I've been staying here, staying there. Then it just got real bad. The drugs and stuff. My kids ... well, they got 'em and put 'em in my husband's family. For a couple of years. Three years." Marion provided a rough estimate: "Six, seven years." Helen similarly provided an approximation: "Maybe three years."

When asked about length of current homelessness, fourteen participants stated they had been homeless for a period of greater than ten years. When such responses were received, the interviewer clarified that this was in one continuous block of time and not broken up with periods of being stably housed. Dale was one of these fourteen women. She had been living on the streets for twelve years, with only one six-month period during which she had resided in a shelter.

---

3 MATTS is a Detroit-area hostel operated by the Salvation Army.
4 A three-quarter house provides transitional living accommodations for the newly sober.

Lastly, eight participants did not answer this question. In a handful of cases we were unable to record a woman's length of current homelessness because she simply did not want to provide an answer. In other situations, length of current homelessness was not recorded because as soon as the interview began, the individual immediately launched into her story and the interviewer was forced to break in at certain points in order to go back and ask for demographic information or to try to pick that information out of the content of what was being shared. In the interest of focusing on what the participants wanted to discuss, when such situations arose, some demographic information was lost.

Homelessness

Pathways into homelessness vary widely, often the result of combinations of structural and interpersonal factors (Hudson et al. 2010; Ellen and O'Flaherty 2010; Shinn 2010). One of the questions we sought to explore with participants revolved around the factors that led to their entry into homelessness. What their answers revealed is that, in a majority of cases, women in this study became homeless through processes over which they felt they had little or no control.

Among younger women, homelessness was often a result of family disputes, usually between the young woman and one or more parents, but this is hardly unique to our sample (Hyde 2005). While the nature of many of the disputes remained nonviolent, this was not uniformly the case and some women reported leaving home as adolescents or young adults due to incidents of neglect, emotional and psychological abuse, and physical and sexual violence by other family members. For older women, disputes with immediate or extended family members, or a partner's relatives, were also cited as causes. For example, Eleanor and her husband became homeless for the first time after leaving their home state to move to California to live with her husband's aunt. Once they were in California to make their fresh start, the aunt changed her mind and asked them to leave on the grounds that she did not have enough room. Without jobs or funds, Eleanor's family was left stranded.

Intimate partner violence (IPV) is a common cause of women's homelessness (Tischler, Rademeyer, and Vostanis 2007), thus it was of little surprise to discover that several women had become homeless after fleeing abusive partners. Nicole, a mother of five, fled her Texas home to enter a shelter in Detroit after her husband had become addicted to prescription pills and became abusive. "I left him because of domestic violence," she explained. Holly first became homeless at age seventeen, when she fled with her two children to a battered woman's shelter because, she said, of "domestic relations with my kids' father."

Several of the women became homeless because of economic circumstances. Stacey, a fifty-four-year-old Los Angeles resident, became homeless for the first time at the age of fifty-two when her unemployment benefits ran out. Likewise, fifty-four-year-old Dagmar, who self-described as one of the "economically displaced people," said of her entry into homelessness six months previously, "I don't think this happened because there's anything wrong with me. I had a job. I've had jobs. The problem is the economy." Camelia was laid off from a doctor's office and, without savings or family members to rely on, found herself in a shelter. Nadia had been on the verge of quitting her contract position to start a clothing store in the Sunset Strip district of Los Angeles when the individual putting up the financing for her entrepreneurial venture backed out of the arrangement, leaving her in debt over store repairs and with a job from which she was laid off two days later. Becky, who had been homeless off and on for the past four years, lost her home when the Social Security Administration took away her Social Security Income (SSI) benefits. Arlene was one of several women who had come to Los Angeles to start a new life but soon found themselves homeless. Simone had also moved to Los Angeles from St. Louis in order to "start all over again." Based on the belief that "there's just more opportunity" in Los Angeles, she had been homeless for the past six months and living in a temporary shelter in Los Angeles's Skid Row district.

Some women found themselves in economically precarious circumstances after the death of a loved one, usually a male partner or parent. For example, Dawn's husband had been the sole provider for the family and, when he died, she "couldn't pay the rent." Lisa, who was also battling a series of serious physical and mental health concerns, including cancer, was placed in a similar situation when her husband and remaining family members died, leaving her without financial support. Priscilla had been a full-time caretaker for her mother; thus, when asked how she had first become homeless, she replied, "I lost my mom. That's how I lost my job." Sixty-year-old Ruby had been financially ruined as a result of having to cover expenses for her critically ill sister, who subsequently passed away. "I had to pay for her hospitalization, her funeral, everything."

1.1. Economic devastation, Detroit. Photo: L. Huey, 2011.

Other women attributed their homelessness to issues with mental health. Sabrina, a fifty-five-year-old New Yorker, had become homeless most recently some six months earlier, when she moved to California to pursue her dreams of becoming a famous singer and marrying the rapper Sean Combs (P. Diddy). First describing her journey as a "spiritual sabbatical," Sabrina later acknowledged that her homelessness was the result of an ongoing struggle with mental health issues diagnosed as schizoaffective disorder. Theresa, who had been a full-time caregiver for her mother, fell into a deep depression following her mother's death and "lost everything," including her will to live, resulting in the loss of her home and being hospitalized multiple times. Jenny, who is also struggling with chronic depression, lost her rental apartment when she was hospitalized for inpatient psychiatric treatment.

Some women attributed their homelessness to drug and alcohol abuse. When Jody, a forty-six-year-old Detroit woman who has been homeless off and on for the past twenty years, was asked how she first came to be homeless, she simply replied, "Alcohol, drugs." This was also the case with Sharleen, who said, "Drugs and alcohol," and Carmela, who replied, "Eviction, addiction." Wendy similarly attributed her homelessness to the fact that she had never held a job because she "was a drug addict." Stephanie was proud of the fact that she had "maintained a pretty good job history," but acknowledged that she had stopped working, and thus had "started getting involved in drugs."

Similar to other studies, many of our participants experienced multiple episodes of homelessness (e.g., Tutty et al. 2013). Some of our participants had been homeless two or three times previously, like Dale, who had kicked her abusive husband out of the family home for "beating on me" in 2004 and was unable to make ends meet on her own. Gloria had also been previously homeless. Having been evicted over drug use, the forty-four-year-old woman had spent a year sleeping in abandoned buildings throughout Chicago. For Gloria, sleeping in what she termed "squalors" was preferable to going to a shelter, because most of the area shelters had a "turn out" policy, which requires clients to be out on the streets at six in the morning. Sheran was on her third episode of homelessness, each time returning to the same shelter. Previously addicted to drugs, but now clean, Sheran had recently returned to the shelter after leaving a supportive living facility because the rent was too high, and after spending some time moving between hotels and the street. Cynthia was now on her fourth period of homelessness, which she attributed to a cycle of imprisonment: "There's been a couple times, like four, because I have been to prison and I was homeless in between." When asked about her own experience of homelessness, Diane described it as "off and on for years." She considered this persistent cycle to be the product of domestic violence: "First time I was homeless I was in an abuse situation … it just spiralled from there. Once you become a battered person, it's likely you'll be homeless every year and it seems like every other year, I just can't get it together."

Violence

Violence is pervasive in the lives of homeless citizens, but this is especially so for homeless women (Baker, Cook, and Norris 2003). Homeless women are far more likely than other populations to be a victim of violence during childhood or adulthood, or both. Some researchers have reported that as many as 80 per cent of women within this segment of the population have been victimized in their lives, often by a family member or intimate partner (Jasinski et al., 2010; Salomon,

Table 1.4. Types of violence experienced

Types of violence	N*
During childhood/adolescence	
Sexual abuse	90
Physical abuse	88
Gang-related violence	28
Witnessed significant violence	51
During adulthood	
Intimate partner violence	126
Sexual assault	92
Physical assault (by a non-intimate partner)	88
Gang-related violence	63
Witnessed significant violence	32

*N here refers to the number of women reporting each form of violence experienced; participants had often experienced more than one form of violence (see also Table 1.5).

Bassuk, and Huntington 2002). In a survey of nearly 1,000 homeless women residing in dozens of shelters or using meal programs in Los Angeles County, Wenzel, Leake, and Gelberg (2001) found that more than one-third of the women had experienced *major* violence in the past year alone (see also Huey, Fthenos, and Hryniewicz 2012). In fact, Wenzel and colleagues concluded that the average homeless woman in the Los Angeles area had experienced as much major violence in just one year as the average American woman experiences in her lifetime.

Victimization in childhood and adolescence was common among the women interviewed. Sexual abuse was the most frequently reported (see Table 1.4), followed closely by physical abuse. As we will discuss in more detail in the next chapter, it was not uncommon for women to report multiple episodes of sexual abuse by different perpetrators or to state they had been victims of both physical and sexual abuse. Further, given the rates of physical abuse in the early homes of participants, we were not surprised to discover that many had also observed significant violence against others, most frequently occurring within the home. Several of the women also reported experiences of gang-related violence, usually as a result of gang affiliation or membership.

In adulthood, the most frequently reported form of violent victimization was IPV. The majority of women in our sample reported one or more episodes of this form of interpersonal violence over the course of their lives. In adulthood, sexual assault was the second most frequently reported form of interpersonal violence experienced, closely followed by physical assaults perpetrated by someone who was not in an

Table 1.5. Multiple types of violence reported

Number of types of violence	N
1	33
2	33
3	36
4	21
5	37
6	18
7	6
8	2
9	1
Total	187

intimate relationship with the victim. This latter category, for instance, includes robberies, random attacks and assaults perpetrated by friends, acquaintances or strangers. As adults, a number of the women had observed significant violence, from serous physical assaults to homicides and others had been a victim of gang-related violence.

Many women experienced multiple types of interpersonal violence. As can be seen in Table 1.5, approximately two-thirds of our participants had been the victims of three or more different types of violence over the course of their lives. Of those who reported experiencing only one or two types of violent victimization, most were survivors of domestic abuse. Consistent with the findings of other studies (e.g., Hudson et al. 2010), many of these women experienced violence in both childhood and adolescence.

Resilience, Strength, and Coping

Given the various life stressors experienced by homeless women – which include not only the process of becoming homeless but also the adversities faced once unhoused – the ways in which these women cope is an important area of investigation. While previous researchers have attempted to understand how women cope with homelessness (Epel, Bandura, and Zimbardo 1999; Finfgeld-Connett 2010), there has been less attention paid to how many women within this situation also deal with the after-effects of violence.[5] We know that being forced to

---

5 Notable examples of work in this area include Milburn, Norweeta, and D'Ercole (1991), and Boes and van Wormer (1997).

move into the precarious social and physical spaces typically inhabited by homeless citizens is a devastating experience (Deck and Platt 2015). We also know that, for many, the resulting loss of social status and stigmatization can be traumatic (S. Thompson et al. 2013). The women in this book had experienced all of this, but also had to deal with both past and relatively recent experiences of violent victimization. As many of these women made clear, and which we document more fully in upcoming chapters, violent victimization frequently left emotional and mental wounds. Indeed, many openly admitted they were traumatized by their experiences, and the result of their traumatic experiences were a host of mental, emotional, social, familial, and interpersonal problems, including symptoms of depression and anxiety, substance abuse, severed relationships, profound distrust, social isolation, and, in some instances, a worsening of long-standing mental health issues.

The ability of homeless women to respond in what might be seen as positive or productive ways to what many of our interviewees acknowledged as manifestations of trauma is circumscribed by three factors. First, homelessness is an all-encompassing, and indeed frequently overwhelming, state for the individual. Most women in this book were eager, in some cases understandably frantic, to get out of their current environment and into secure housing. The struggle to get out of shelters, tents, and alleys meant that individual efforts were directed largely, if not solely, at exiting homelessness, typically through securing housing, employment, or schooling. Thus, responding to any emotional or mental after-effects of violence was seen as secondary importance, and, in some instances, as detrimental to the goal of "getting out." A common response, then, was suppression, or to become, as Tonya said, "numb" or "hard to [one's] emotions" by blocking out both memories and feelings that might disrupt one's ability to get out of her current situation. A second factor is the environment itself and the physical insecurity found within the streets and other spaces within which homeless citizens are forced to live (Huey 2012). Many of the women could not escape reminders of violence, and the fears and anxieties that violence can instill, because they were living in spaces that offered them daily reminders of their susceptibility to victimization. Several women reported, for example, witnessing acts of violence while out on the streets, whereas others cited specific examples of their own victimization while homeless, including acts of random violence from passers-by, as well as sexual assaults and beatings from street-based friends, acquaintances, and strangers. A third, and equally important factor, is the lack of quality psychological services for homeless citizens. While the availability of services varies widely within and across the three cities in which this work was conducted – Detroit, Chicago, and Los Angeles – several of the shelters and other facilities visited offered no counselling services (either on-site or off-site). Even when services are available, as the authors have documented elsewhere (Huey et al., 2014), shelter and other service workers often do not ask about victimization during intake, and thus women are often not referred to counselling. Where services are available and accessible, they are often vulnerable to budget cuts. For example, while conducting field work in Los Angeles, counselling services at one site were in the process of being cut due to budget restrictions, and counsellors and other employees at the site were leaving.

We highlight the issues above because it is imperative to understand that resilience and coping are context-specific phenomena. Thus, what might appear to be struggling, or basic survival, in one situation can, in an unconventional setting such as the streets, be examples of personal strength and demonstrative of one's resolve to overcome adversity, including past traumas, and therefore constitute perfectly appropriate responses given a lack of alternatives. The term some researchers have coined for this phenomenon is "hidden resilience" (Ungar 2004, 2006).

In his work on homeless youth, Michael Ungar (2004, 2006) has observed that popular or mainstream conceptions of what constitutes "healthy functioning" are often not culturally sensitive. In writing on individuals termed "troubled children," he describes, for example, how culturally sensitive approaches to understanding how these individuals can function within adverse spaces or situations can reveal hidden struggles to overcome hardship. In their struggles, he argues, these young people are not only developing resilience but also are attempting to fashion new, more powerful identities and stronger senses of self. As Ungar explains:

> Why is it that some children, despite experiencing adversity, manage to bounce back in what we consider positive, socially acceptable ways such as maintaining good grades or not getting into trouble? We call these children resilient. But resilience, the capacity to overcome adversity, is not just a measure of how well some children behave in ways we approve of. The paradox is that resilience is equally present in young people whom we have labelled as dangerous, delinquent, deviant and/or disordered. Resilient youth take advantage of whatever opportunities and resources

that are available – even those we consider negative or destructive. That negative behaviour shown in troubled young people can actually signal a pathway to hidden resilience that is, just like the one chosen by their well-behaved peers, simply focused on the need to create powerful and influential identities for themselves. (2005, 1)

It is not simply that researchers are beginning to re-examine what might otherwise be termed individual "pathology" or "dysfunction" in light of where people are socially situated. Researchers are also, and perhaps most importantly for our own analysis, re-examining resilience in relation to what victims and traumatized groups say about themselves and how they self-identify in terms of overcoming past and present experiences of violence, economic adversity, and other painful issues (Sanders, Munford, and Liebenberg 2012). To illustrate, drawing on girls' own narratives, Hine and Welford (2012) have used the concept of hidden resilience to explore the instrumental use of violence by girls as a response to living within environments in which they are heavily marginalized. Harvey (2012) has similarly employed hidden resilience as a construct in both her therapeutic and research work with GLBTQ youth. As Harvey notes, young people's sexual identity is a source of marginalization that can, "it stands to reason," lead some youth to seek "unconventional ways ... to protect them and promote their own growth" (2012, 328–9). Perhaps not surprisingly, "these strategies [are] typically viewed as problematic by families, schools, religious groups, and others, [but] may in fact be valid self-driven attempts to succeed and grow in unsupportive cultures and contexts" (2012, 329).

In the pages that follow, we draw on Ungar's (2004, 2006) approach to better understand how the women we have interviewed – individuals who are struggling with multiple forms of adversity, including the after-effects of violence – view themselves in terms of the process of becoming resilient. Rather than adopting a maternalistic or paternalistic approach to understanding and categorizing their subjective experiences, we choose to let the women speak for themselves and to tell us how they self-identify.

You've Got to Be "Strong"

A conventional way in which researchers might ask individuals about where they are in terms of developing resilience after a traumatic event would be to ask something like, "Do you see yourself as having become

Table 1.6. Resilience self-identification

Extent of resilience	N
Resilient (strong)	168
Weak	14
Mixed feelings/unsure	5
Total	187

more resilient?" Others may assess resilience according to standardized scales that attempt to measure aspects of this construct. Our experience is that neither approach works very well with highly marginalized people. In many instances, interviewees in our studies did not understand what the term "resilient" meant, and most psychological scales are not normed for use with homeless populations.

As noted in the introduction, our approach was to use qualitative interviewing, beginning with a series of exploratory, open-ended questions not only about mental and emotional distress but also about the extent to which these women saw themselves in the process of becoming resilient. To do so, we phrased our questions using their own language, as discovered through analysis of our earliest interviews. As will be recalled, in these first interviews, women frequently used the terms "strong" or "survivor," as well as "moving on" or "getting over it" (see Huey, Fthenos, and Hryniewicz, 2012). In *all* subsequent interviews, we therefore avoided psychological constructs and terms in favour of asking participants directly how they saw themselves and to what extent they self-identified as "strong" versus "vulnerable" or "weak."

The women in this study overwhelmingly saw themselves as either becoming resilient or as having achieved resilience (see Table 1.6). Maggie, who has experienced a lifetime of childhood physical abuse, domestic violence, and sexual assault, represents a case in point:

> I consider myself a big survivor. Extremely strong. I know that nothing can get me down. I know that giving up … I cannot give up. I have to keep on pushing it and moving on. There's a bigger picture here. I know that this was not meant for me to be in. There's something bigger planned for me. I feel it in my heart. I'm going for it. That's why I believe in being positive all the time. You must be positive. You must at all times. When you constantly dwell on negative things, bad things will always happen. It's a state of mind in here. I used to be that type of person, to hold onto

things, that people hurt me or this bad thing happened over whatever, I had to learn from experience. It took many years. You have to let that stuff go. That's the past, just move onto the future.

Rosa, who at thirty-two years old was one of the women who had experienced seven different types of interpersonal violence, is currently in therapy trying to rebuild her life. When asked if she sees herself as "strong," she replied, "I have to be. I'm in this world all by myself." Several of the women did not just see themselves as "strong" but as "very strong." One of these individuals was Renisa, a mother of seven children, who had spent two-and-a-half years trying to raise her children while living in and out of motels. "I'm very strong … a lot of people ask me, 'How'd you do it?'"

Some of the women's responses to this category of questions, like that provided by Rosa, indicated that they saw themselves as having innate personal strength that they could draw upon as needed. Jean is another individual who saw herself as being strong out of necessity: "I have to." Others, like Maggie, provided answers that revealed that they had developed that personal strength through a process of becoming increasingly resilient. Amy is in this latter group. When asked if she sees herself as "strong," she responded: "I do." However, she subsequently indicated that this was not always the case, and that she had previously been a "big softie," who had had difficulties overcoming both a sexual assault and an addiction. Having begun the process of working on both of these issues, she saw herself as strong "at this point in time." This was also the case for Denise, who had survived physical and sexual assaults in both childhood and as an adult. "As of now, yes," she said, when asked this same question. Ruby had a similar response, but expanded a bit more fully on her process: "I survived. I've been surviving and I'm going to keep surviving. I've become very strong through all the things that have happened to me. Living here I've learned a lot. I'm seeing, listening, watching." Chantelle, who survived childhood physical and sexual abuse, as well as IPV, sees herself as being on a journey to which she remains committed: "I don't want to give up. I know that I am capable of some great things. So, I just have to be strong and keep doing it. I'll get there. I've been there and I've fallen down … but, I'm going to pull through it."

Researchers who work within street-based cultures are familiar with the concept of "fronting." Fronting is a protective measure in which individuals adopt tough, street-wise personas in order to avoid possible predation from others who might see them as weak or vulnerable (Anderson 1999; Mullins and Cardwell-Mullins 2006; Froyum 2013; Huey and Quirouette 2010; Huey 2016). Saying one is strong when they are in fact feeling weak, and adopting an appropriate tough guise to back up such statements, is not uncommon. Therefore, we cannot rule out the possibility that some of our participants were "fronting" during interviews and saying they were stronger than they felt. However, as one of the authors has documented elsewhere (Huey 2016), as time went on and trust was established between the participant and interviewer, some of these women did, indeed, drop their tough guise and reveal their vulnerabilities, expressing pain, uncertainty, doubts, and insecurities over both their present and future ability to "get over it."

Another phenomenon deserving consideration is the "strong black woman" stereotype. This stereotype has been described as a perception that black women are "naturally strong, resilient, self-contained, and self-sacrificing" (Donovan and West 2015, 384). As we have noted, most participants were African American and most women self-identified as "strong." In one of our first interviews, one of the authors explored this stereotype by asking a woman in Chicago if she felt pressure to pretend to be strong in order to adhere to this set of beliefs about "how black women should be." Her response:

> MARIAH: I feel like that if I was any other colour, I still need to be strong.
> INTERVIEWER: It's about you?
> MARIAH: Right. It's not about the colour. I hate when people do that, when they colourize situations. Nah. Don't do that! It's not the fact that you're black. It's not the fact that you're white. It's the fact that you're a strong woman. If you're gonna be that woman, do it because you are that strong woman, not because of what race you is. What's that gotta do with it?

Although this was not a standard question we asked all women of colour, the topic did arise in subsequent discussions, and was just as quickly rejected as a salient factor for explaining women's sense of personal strength.

Besides, not all women self-identified as strong. Heidi was one of these women. When she was asked if she feels strong, Heidi shook her head. "No," and explained, "my dad was taken from me [murdered] at twenty-five and I've never gotten over that." Tonya, who had spent years on the streets, and was battling major depression after years of trauma, saw herself as weak because "strength comes from not allowing things to affect you." She also saw herself as a compassionate person and, echoing "street code" (Anderson 1999), felt this compassion for others made her vulnerable: "It's also a hindrance. It makes you weak." Sunny acknowledged having mixed feelings when asked about her ability to remain strong and overcome her emotional and other scars. "Down and up," she said. "It depends … every day is not a good day, because you're always fighting with yourself about different things that's going on with you." Benita, who has been struggling with addiction, on top of the traumatic effects of IPV and sexual assault, carries guilt and shame associated with her victimization and subsequent drug use. When asked if she would consider herself a strong individual, she replied, "Yeah, I guess. Not really, but maybe." After a brief discussion of how normal it is for victims of violence to experience many of the same feelings she has, the extent to which she had been carrying shame became fully apparent: "Now I feel a bit of relief, because I don't feel so different from everybody else. I guess I don't need to have as much shame as I do."

Conclusions

In this chapter, we have provided a general overview of the women whose experiences inform this book. They varied in race and age, and in their experiences with homelessness. While some had been homeless for as little as one day at the time of the interviews, others had been homeless for more than a decade; while some are experiencing homelessness as a transition following a disruptive life event, others are consistently or chronically homeless. Some were homeless for the first time, but others had experienced many, many episodes of homelessness.

Several studies have shown the pervasive and serious violence experienced by homeless women (Huey, Fthenos, and Hryniewicz, 2012; Jasinski et al. 2010). For many women, this violence begins in childhood and continues throughout their adult lives. Like many women who are not homeless, much of this violence occurs at the hands of somebody within their social network, such as a parent, other family member, or partner (Browne and Bassuk 1997; Tischler Rademeyer, and Vostanis, 2007). Indeed, many homeless women's lives are filled with experiences of physical and sexual assault in childhood and adulthood, IPV, and gang violence; when they aren't being abused themselves, many women witness severe violence.

Despite their experiences with homelessness and violence, 90 per cent of the women interviewed self-identified as strong, and their words reveal they saw themselves as either resilient (having "moved on") or in the process of becoming resilient ("moving on"). Several also stated they were proud of the adversity they have overcome and were actively working to build better lives for themselves. In the chapters that follow, we will explore these women's experiences of violence, as well as the traumatic after-effects of those experiences, before examining the resources and coping strategies upon which they draw in order to keep "moving on."

Chapter Two

Victimization

I was getting very bad flashbacks to what happened with me when I lived with this man. He was creepy. Creepy. He scared me down to my soul.

– Gillian

Like many of the women in this book, Gillian had an extensive history of violent victimization, the beginnings of which she traced to a relationship with her ex-husband, the man she described as scaring her "down to [her] soul." Gillian's marriage, which she spoke of as being "a little abusive," became completely dysfunctional when Gillian was introduced to crack cocaine, which her husband used to control her.

> I don't know what he was into or what was up, but I knew that there were always baseballs of crack. There are so many things I don't remember, so many times where I woke up in places that it would scare me. I don't know if I was blacking out or what I was doing during those times … He abused me something terrible. He hurt me deeply on a physical level, spiritual level, psychological level. Every level.

Once Gillian was addicted to crack, she lost custody of her two children. She also endured emotional abuse from a husband who "hated her" and repeatedly told her she was "going to die in the gutter." The relationship ended when he threw her out of the house.

Individuals who lack resources and support, like Gillian, often turn to sex work to meet basic needs. This work, in turn, places them at increased risk of violence (Kurtz et al. 2004). Gillian was revictimized while working the streets. She was kidnapped by a john who physically and sexually assaulted her. She described this terrifying experience as follows: "I was raped and he stuck stuff in me. He gouged out my skin with a screw driver [lifts sleeve to show scars]. Then he put me in a trunk for three days, naked, bleeding. It was not good. The amazing thing is that he let me go." As Gillian's experience exemplifies, the streets can be a dangerous environment for unhoused women (Wardhaugh 1999). Women in various studies have reported experiencing physical and sexual violence, including having been stabbed, burned, shot, strangled, and beaten (Jasinski et al. 2010; Huey 2016). In addition, the spaces in which homeless citizens inhabit also make it more likely they will witness violence (Harley and Hunn 2015). These experiences often combine into a lifelong history of polyvictimization, as homeless women also frequently report high rates of violent victimization in childhood and in adulthood prior to and after episodes of homelessness (Huey and Ricciardelli 2016).

Our sample consists of women who experienced at least one form of violent victimization in their lives; however, as we documented in the previous chapter, many had been victimized in multiple ways. In this chapter, we provide greater detail of women's victimization histories. We begin by examining physical and sexual abuse experienced in childhood. We then turn to women's experiences dealing with intimate partner violence (IPV), an especially common form of victimization among women in general, and homeless women in particular. Next, we detail women's experiences with sexual and non-intimate partner physical violence in adulthood, before discussing participants' experiences witnessing violence and with gang violence in both childhood and adulthood.

Childhood Physical Abuse

Childhood physical violence is a frequent precursor to adolescent and adult homelessness (Browne 1993; Davies-Netzley, Hurlburt, and Hough 1996; Jasinski et al. 2010; Green et al. 2012). Researchers have also identified links between exposure to childhood maltreatment and violent victimization in adulthood (Wesely and Wright 2009; Huey, Fthenos, and Hryniewicz 2012; Edalati, Krausz, and Schutz 2016). We found both: high rates of childhood physical abuse and patterns of victimization later in life. In this section, we explore the former, by revealing women's narratives of abuse.

Jacqui, age eighteen, found herself pregnant and living in a Detroit shelter as a result of ongoing physical and sexual abuse. Of the physical violence she had experienced, she said, "My mama, she used to beat me all the time. With poles. Extension cords. All that stuff." Nineteen-year-old Mariah had been placed into foster care at the age of twelve because of "child abuse and neglect." Of the child abuse, she said, "My momma used to stomp my head in." Sheran, who said she was beat with "whips on my back, on my face, arms, legs ... just because" by her mother, was also the recipient of a torrent of verbal and emotional abuse: "[She'd] tell me that I would not be anything." Patti's mother, who she describes as "hav[ing] some mental issues," used to beat her as a child for soiling her bed. Describing the beatings inflicted by her mother, Patti said, "[It] was extreme."

In some cases, women reported experiencing physical abuse from parents well into adulthood. Caprice, for example, grew up with a mother she described as "a mean drunk." When asked if she had ever experienced physical abuse in childhood, she replied, "So as far as child abuse, knowing what I know now ... yeah." Terra similarly grew up with an alcoholic mother she described as "physical." Brittney related that not only had she "experienced physical abuse from my mother growing up," but that, as an adult, she remained in a verbally and emotionally abusive relationship with her mother: "Even today she was on the phone on me. All I did was say, 'Mama, can I come over there?' And she yelled at me, 'You gotta get your stuff right now. I am tired of you.'" Melania's experience of physical abuse from her mother continued into early adulthood. Now twenty-three years old, Melania was last assaulted by her mother when Melania was seven months pregnant and "she kicked me in my stomach."

Fathers and stepfathers were also responsible for physical abuse women had experienced. Fifty-three-year-old Eve grew up in a violent family in Chicago, with a father who "whupped me. Busted my skin, had marks, stuff like that." Kim described a hellish life in her childhood home with a violent stepfather: "It was hitting, punching and throwing glasses of pop. It was knives being thrown and guns being put to your head. Pistol whipped and stuff because you don't want to do what they want you to do." Angela's exposure to violence began with watching her father beat her mother, violence that was subsequently directed at her: "First it was my dad and my mom, but when I turned thirteen, it was me and him." Eleanor was sent to live with a physically abusive father after she revealed to her disbelieving mother that her mother's boyfriend had been sexually abusing her.

Sometimes both parents in the home were physically abusive. Celine said of her early life, "I had it very rough. My parents ... they were very physical." She added, "A lot of stuff was really, really awful." Marlys was physically abused by a stepfather, who "beat me with an extension cord until I passed out. I was out of school for a month because I had cuts on my arm, all over the inside of my face." Her mother was no less abusive. Of her mother, Marlys told the following story to illustrate the verbal, emotional and physical abuse she was subjected to:

> When she punished me and I went against her punishment, she would put me out of the house with no place to go. It got to the point where I felt uncomfortable talking to her. She told me she would get me birth control pills if I wanted to have sex. When I told her I wanted those pills, she beat me up and told me I was a bitch.

As a result of abuse, parental abandonment, neglect, or other problems within families of origin, many women were removed from their family home as children and placed into the foster care system or with other family members. According to the most recent data from the U.S. Department of Health and Human Services, on any single day more than 400,000 youth are in foster care, and more than 250,000 young people enter care annually. Of those in foster care in America, about one-quarter are placed with relatives (Child Welfare Information Gateway 2015). Upon discovery of abuse or neglect, several of the women in this study were removed from the homes of their primary caregiver and sent to live with other family members – as happened to Eleanor – or were placed within the foster care system. Sheran, for example, was sent to live with her grandmother. Jasmine was raised by a physically abusive grandmother, who would dole out a "severe whupping" whenever Jasmine got into trouble. Jasmine illustrated the nature of what one of those whuppings entailed: "One time she tried to whup me with an extension cord and I ducked and it hit me in the side of the face and caught this much of my skin." Thus, whereas some noted that the removal, despite the fact it was undoubtedly a traumatic experience, placed them within a better environment, others continued to experience abuse. Michaele was raised by an aunt who was physically and emotionally abusive. "For a long time, I thought she was my mother," Michaele informed us, adding, "the bubble got busted when [my aunt said], 'I'm not your mother and I'm not your friend and I really don't like you.'" Seven referenced both the physical abuse and neglect she experienced as a child being raised by "Aunties," who "really just wanted me for the money."

Childhood Sexual Abuse

It was also not uncommon for women to share stories of sexual abuse experienced in childhood. Male relatives were most frequently the perpetrators, with several of the women stating they had been sexually abused by uncles and/or family friends whom they knew as "uncles." From the ages of twelve to fourteen, Nadja said her uncle would "park the car behind the liquor store and stick his tongue down my throat and feel my breasts. Tried to put his hands between my legs." Wendy, who was sexually abused by an uncle, believes that the abuse began when she was two or three years old. She was not his only victim: "He did it to me and to my two cousins." Briana revealed that she had been sexually abused by not one but two different uncles. Jacqui had been continually sexually abused throughout her childhood by her mother's boyfriends, resulting in a pregnancy. She was forced to leave home when she confronted her mother:

> I got into it with her boyfriend. He told me that if he wasn't with her, he'd be with me. And I brung it to her attention. She didn't believe me. She brung it to his attention. She done said, "Your daddy ain't gonna do nothing to you, you know that." But that's not my daddy ... we got into an argument. I was pregnant. He told me he would throw me out the window and all this stuff.

When Paula was asked if she had ever been sexually abused as a child, she replied: "My father ... he touched me." As an adolescent, Dee was sexually assaulted in two separate foster homes, by both foster brothers and foster fathers. Cherie was also sexually assaulted in foster care by a foster father, whom she described as also physically abusive. Kim was sexually abused by her stepfather: "I have an eight-year-old son from a rape, when I was a child. I was molested and raped all the way from the age of nine to seventeen, when I got pregnant. It was hard because I had to live in the house with the person because they supposed to raise me as their daughter." Kelly was physically abused by her mother and "raped by her boyfriend." Anisha, then eight years old, was sexually abused by her brother and his friend. When she reported it to her mother, she was forced to take a pregnancy test. After the test result turned out to be negative, she was told, "Okay, we're never going to speak about this again."

Victims rarely disclose childhood sexual abuse as it happens –
about two-thirds of adults who retrospectively report being sexually assaulted in childhood did not tell anybody about their abuse as
children (London et al. 2005). When child sexual abuse is reported,
it is often done months, or even years, after the incident occurred
(London et al. 2005). When a family member is the perpetrator, disclosure is often further delayed (Goodman-Brown et al. 2003). Given
low rates of disclosure, one would hope that those young people
who do come forward are taken seriously and that their reports are
duly acted upon. This does not always seem to be the case, though
(Elliott and Carnes 2001). Many of the women in our study who
disclosed childhood sexual abuse fell into the latter category. Anisha's experience, described above, was not that unusual, as other
women reported similar responses when they told family members
about sexual abuse. For example, when Kendra told her aunt that
her aunt's boyfriend had molested her, the aunt "brushed it off."
After Brittney told her mother that she was being sexually abused
by a cousin, "she kept sending me over" to the houses where it was
happening. Today, Brittney says, "I hate her for that." Even though
Eleanor was placed into foster care as a result of sexual abuse by
her stepfather that occurred between the ages of eight and fifteen,
her mother "insisted that I was lying." Amina said she "had a rough
childhood ... I couldn't go out and jump rope with the other kids.
I was stuck in the house. Through grammar school, high school."
During that entire period, Amina and her sister were being sexually
abused by her stepfather. When asked if her mother ever knew what
was happening, Amina replied, "No, she really wasn't paying it no
attention until I let it out." As adults, Amina and her sister revealed
the abuse to a disbelieving mother. Amina was herself disbelieving
of her mother's inability to have figured out what had been happening: "At seventeen, I'm pregnant and I don't have a boyfriend. I'm
not hanging out with friends. And my mom never looked at that. He
drove me to school, picked me up at school, so how did I get pregnant? Inside this house."

In a handful of cases, women were sexually assaulted by strangers or other non-family members. Denise's mother sent her and
her brother to the laundromat. Once there, a man lured the fifteen-
year-old outside and started to drag her down an alley. "He took my
clothes off and told me that if I told anyone, he would kill me and my
brother."

Intimate Partner Violence (IPV)

Homeless women are over-represented among victims of IPV (Browne and Bassuk 1997; Wenzel et al. 2001). Further, IPV is itself a significant cause of women's homelessness (Netto, Pawson, and Sharp 2009; Baker et al. 2010). This is no less the case with respect to the women in this study, the majority of whom reported experiencing one or more abusive intimate relationships.

From the outside, Leah lived what appeared to be the picture-perfect life with a successful husband and beautiful home. "We had this image," she said, "that we were this perfect entity." The reality was very different: "There were times when we were travelling around the world and times when he would put a knife to my throat. After the second and third time, I realized he wasn't bullshitting. He really was gonna kill me." Leah fled to a domestic violence shelter, because, she said, "I didn't want to be a statistic." When she was barely out of adolescence, Tiffany began a relationship with a forty-eight-year-old man. "We used to fight all time," she said. "Do everything but break bones." During one fight, "he put a butcher knife up to my neck and he had said, 'I will kill you if you keep on doing something.' He threatened to kill me a couple of times." During another fight, he "literally hit me in the back of the head with a broomstick handle." Like many women in her situation (Davies, Ford-Gilbe, and Hammerton 2009; Eckstein 2011), Tiffany said she "was too afraid to leave the relationship because I didn't really have any other place to go. So, I just stayed."

As can be seen from the stories our participants shared, the level of violence experienced was sometimes extreme. Jasmine said her ex-boyfriend "tried to set me on fire with a blowtorch." Jenny's first husband would lock her in the basement overnight and make her stand in the corner on one leg. "Every time my leg would drop, he'd hit me." Over the course of eight years of abuse, he also repeatedly raped her. Brittney's ex-partner, who was himself an addict, introduced her to cocaine and heroin and fuelled her addiction by actively undermining her attempts at getting off drugs. He also beat her savagely when she failed to give him money for his own drugs. Charity was chased by an ex-husband who was wielding a knife and threatening to "torture" her. Arlene experienced two miscarriages as a result of savage beatings she received by her ex-husband. Kim noted that when she attempted to leave her abusive husband after seventeen years of marriage, "he tried to kill me." Michaele had been in two physically abusive relationships. The first one she described by saying, "A couple of scabs here and there, a busted lip. No, no black eyes. Nothing ever got broken." In the second relationship, she said, a boyfriend "tried to choke me to death."

Some of the women reported being stalked by violent ex-partners. Jenny repeatedly left her violent ex-husband. Her attempts at leaving him were, however, confounded by his ability to find her. Once located, he "would push his way in. Tie me up. Rape me. Beat me." After another unsuccessful attempt at hiding from him, he started harassing Jenny by making torches with gasoline soaked rags on them and sticking them through her windows. In her twenties, Amina entered into an abusive relationship with a man who believed that "if you love your woman, you gotta beat 'em!" When she left him, he tracked her. "Every time he saw me on the street, he'd be running for me. He found out where I stayed. I had a new boyfriend at the time. He was throwing big rocks at my windows. Broke all my windows out." Amina became so scared of this man that, at one point, she purchased a gun for self-defence. "If you come back to me," she told him, "I'm going to shoot you."

Sexual Assault

Among our participants, almost half were sexually assaulted in adulthood. Toya, a thirty-four-year-old African American mother living in Chicago, was raped by a non-spouse relative as an adult. Toya's husband's cousin, a man who had been harassing her for sex for some time previously, was the perpetrator. As she explained:

> We was in a buildin' and I goes in the alley to look for him [her husband], because he says he was on his way. His cousin followed me. He's talkin' to me and stuff and I'm like blowin' him off. "I'm straight, I'm straight. Why you still askin' me this? You don't care nothin' bout your cousin?" I'm givin' it to him like that. This man grabs me and takes me under the porch on one of the buildings and raped me.

Clarita, on the other hand, was sexually assaulted by a stranger, a man she had accepted a ride from: "He told me he had a gun under the seat of the car." Sabrina had been "date raped." When Holly was eight months pregnant with her second child, she was also sexually assaulted. She said a stranger entered the room of the place she was staying in and "showed me the .357 [and] put it to my head." At age fifteen, Marlys said she was sexually assaulted by a "guy that I went to high school with." The perpetrator pulled out a gun and proceeded to beat and rape Marlys.

Whereas Toya had been sexually assaulted prior to becoming homeless, other women were raped while sleeping rough, living in a shelter or staying in local hotels. To be sure, sexual victimization is common among those who are homeless. Jasinski et al. (2010) report that homeless women are at least three times more likely than non-homeless women to be raped. In one of the most comprehensive studies of the antecedents of sexual assault for homeless women, Wenzel, Koegel, and Gelberg (2000) found that homeless women who are dependent on drugs, receive income from survival strategies like panhandling or trading sex, live outdoors, have mental health problems, or are physically disabled are much more likely to have been sexually assaulted in the past thirty days than homeless women without these characteristics. Salma was raped when she was squatting in an abandoned Chicago building: "I had my back to the guy, and he just came over and grabbed me, told me to bend over and have sex with him." Gina, who had spent years living on the streets and in parks, said of that time, "A woman on the streets is marked for any predator." To illustrate, she added, "I've been raped." Since Liz has been homeless, she had been raped twice. Tamara, like several other women interviewed, had been sexually assaulted while engaging in sex work. Sex workers, in general, are at an increased risk of being sexually assaulted or raped; being homeless further increases this risk (Shannon et al. 2009). "You're walking out there like a hooker," she said. "You never know who's going to walk up to you, what they might do to you, as far as things like that, or lie to you or rape you or something. I had that happen in my first two years twice." Blue stated she had been raped several times. These assaults occurred when she was "sleeping outside at night" or "prostituting." Of the latter, she said, "I might get into a car with a guy that don't want to pay and then he just takes sex."

It was not unusual for women to state they had been sexually assaulted on multiple occasions (see also Jasinski et al. 2010). For example, when Amber, a fifty-year-old Detroit woman, was asked if she had ever been sexually assaulted, she replied, "Oh yes. It's ironic of you to say this, because I can count on one hand the consensual sex that I've had all my life." Paula estimated that she had "been raped and beat about seven times."

Physical Assault

Although perhaps discussed less frequently within the literature than forms of domestic violence, it is not uncommon for homeless women to experience physical assaults by non-intimate partners (Jasinski et al. 2010). Many of the women in this book, for example, related stories involving physical assaults perpetrated by non-intimate partners. Even still, many of these non-intimate partner assaults were perpetrated by an acquaintance. In Celine's case, the perpetrator was a friend, whom she said "wound up busting my nose." Leilani agreed to have sex with a man she knew from around Skid Row in return for drugs. When she left him without providing the sexual favours promised, the next time he saw her in the street he punched her in the face. Debbie got into a situation that she described as a "physical altercation" with an acquaintance. As she was walking into her building, "he grabbed me by my hair," she related, "and he was going to hit me." Her quick-thinking roommate, who stepped in and pushed her into the building, saved her.

Some women did offer examples of assaults perpetrated by strangers. Jody was randomly assaulted by a homeless male outside of a Detroit area shelter, who hit her in the face with "a real hard blow" for no apparent reason. Sheran was attacked when she became "sick" from withdrawal symptoms and went looking for money for drugs. Using her van for privacy, she picked up a man who became violent and "stabbed [her] about seventeen times in the eye." While pregnant and walking with her children, Meda was assaulted by a gang of robbers: "We got jumped ... I had blood on me." Gianna's robbers also physically attacked her, resulting in a broken jaw. While Angela was in the street looking to score dope, she was "snatched" by a stranger, who attempted to pull her into a nearby alley: "I think his intent was to rape me, but he didn't. We fought." Some women were physically assaulted by strangers simply because they were visibly homeless on the streets. For instance, Jamie, a young Chicago woman who had been living on the streets and in shelters for three years, said that while standing outside of shelters people would sometimes "throw things at me." On one occasion, while sitting outside of a well-known Chicago mission, she recounted, "some dude walking by just threw this weird piece of paper. Crumpled it up and threw it at me."

Witnessing Violence[1]

Most children living in households where at least one parent is abused directly witness the violence (Holt, Buckley, and Whelan 2008). The proportion of children who indirectly witness or are exposed to IPV – such as by overhearing verbal aggression or assaults – is even greater (Holt, Montesinos, and Christensen 2007; Wolak and Finkelhor 1998). About one-quarter of our participants described witnessing violence in childhood or adolescence; usually, they discussed witnessing IPV. As an example, Eve recalled that her father "used to sling my mother around the house ... sling her around the house by her hair." Angela said that her first memory was of "seeing my dad beat the hell out of my mom." Sharleen described an early life with a mother who was "an alcoholic and a drug addict," and having to watch as every one of her mother's boyfriends "beat her." April, aged eighteen years at the time of the interview, described life within a highly dysfunctional family when asked if she had observed much violence in her young life: "Yeah. Unh hunh. Abuse. Gang violence. Fights. And all that."

Children's exposure to community violence has been the focus of considerable research (Fowler et al. 2009). Consistent with social disorganization and routine activities theories, which suggest that low-income communities are beset with problems that increase the likelihood of exposure to violence (Goldner et al. 2011), African American youth in low-income urban neighbourhoods are especially likely to witness violence (Stein et al. 2003). Of the homeless women interviewed, some reported having witnessed significant violence perpetrated by strangers. As a child, Naomi remembered having been "around a tragedy." That tragedy, she related, involved an incident where "a lady got shot in the head." Naomi was standing so near the victim that she could "smell the blood from her being shot." As a child, Margaret had not only seen her parents physically assaulting each other, but "people get killed" in her neighbourhood. When asked to elaborate on this, she responded, "If they were playing a dice game, somebody would get stabbed to death."

---

1 In Table 1.4 in the previous chapter we separated reports of witnessing significant violence according to whether these episodes had occurred in childhood/adolescence or adulthood. In this chapter, we have opted to combine them within one section for ease of reading.

2.1. Drug house,[2] Detroit. Photo: L. Huey, 2011.

Many women witnessed significant violence as adults, too. Sharleen, who grew up in a gang-associated family, stated that later in life she had also seen a high degree of violence associated with local drug activity, including "people get[ting] shot in the neck." On multiple occasions, Tonya has been exposed to the casual violence associated with Detroit's street gang warfare. The first time, she was nearly caught in the crossfire: "They was shooting. Actually shooting across from each other in cars. Out on the streets. Just shooting." Tonya described feeling upset after this incident, but now shrugs and said, "You keep seeing this stuff, you get used to it."

Women in Los Angeles's Skid Row district frequently described witnessing violence. For example, when Eleanor was asked if she had ever

---

2 This abandoned building, located across from a Detroit area youth shelter, is a local drug hangout. Aside from the sign warning "nark[s]" (i.e., snitches) to stay away, another clue as to its use came when one of the authors observed drug deals taking place in front of the building.

observed violence as an adult, she replied, referring to the streets outside the shelter, "You see violence every day ... I saw a fight there the
other day, but I don't hang out there. I don't like it." Dawn's response
to this question was: "Shoo ... yeah, yeah, I see it every day. You don't
need no TV here, man. Go outside for ten, twenty minutes and you
see the reality TV, the soap opera, all the police chases, crime drama,
all that." Similarly, Faith stated that in living on Skid Row, "You see
[violence] every day around here." Rosa noted that she saw "people
get beat up all the time. I see people getting robbed." Sondra also discussed violence on the streets, but also noted that she had witnessed
violence while incarcerated. To illustrate, she revealed that she had
"watched some guy get his head bashed in with weights while we were
in lockup." When asked what had precipitated the assault, she replied,
"[It was] over a name."

Gang Violence

National data collected by the Office of Juvenile Justice and Delinquency
Prevention (OJJDP) show that youth gangs are common in America,
and that they are active in urban, suburban, and rural communities
(Yoder, Whitbeck, and Hoyt 2001; see also Watkins and Taylor 2016).
Gang involvement may be especially appealing to homeless and runaway youth by offering a sort of kinship to individuals who have often
distanced themselves from their family; gangs may also offer some
measure of protection to street youth (Watkins and Taylor 2016). Indeed,
researchers have found that youth who run away at a younger age are
more likely to be involved in gangs than other youth (Yoder, Whitbeck,
and Hoyt 2001). In addition, homeless youth who experienced physical
violence in their family of origin are more likely to report gang involvement (Yoder, Whitbeck, and Hoyt 2001). Not surprisingly, given the violent life histories of the homeless women we interviewed, several of the
younger women, and a handful of the older participants, stated they
had either been associated with gangs or in gangs themselves. Seven
is a young woman with a history of being in gangs in both Detroit and
California. As a teenager, she had been "jumped in by a gang here in
Detroit." At age sixteen, the now twenty-year-old had run away from
a foster home with an older man who forced her into prostitution in
California. While there, she became associated with local gang members, before returning to Detroit. Seven had turned to gangs because of
a need for the social bonds that come from membership. This was also

the case with Jasmine, who said, "I got affiliated with the Blood gang because that's where I felt comforted," and Diane who described herself as "an outsider" until local gang members "took me in."

Through their gang affiliations, Seven and the other women like her, were exposed to both interpersonal violence and gang warfare as victims, bystanders, and perpetrators. Today Jasmine regrets much of what she did as a gang member, which included "setting houses on fire … stealing cars [and] shoot outs." Lake also acknowledged participating in similar activities: "I've been in shootings." Several women told stories of being bystanders to gang-related violence. Candy, who was gang affiliated, was present when gun-related violence broke out between gang members: "I saw my boyfriend get shot in the back three times. I was standing by the shooter." More frequently, though, women reported being victimized as a result of their gang-related activities. For example, although Eve was not a gang member, she was gang associated and one of the functions she served was to "hold the guns." As a result of her affiliation with one Chicago area gang, she was gang raped by members of a rival gang.

Other women were touched by gang violence as a consequence of living in certain neighbourhoods, or because they were simply in the wrong place at the wrong time. Noelle grew up around gang violence in her native Jamaica. Moving to Los Angeles, she found a job as a telemarketer, a job that allowed her to secure apartments in poorer neighbourhoods within the city. As a result, she was often exposed to gang violence, both before and after she became homeless. After Sue left her abusive husband, she was forced to take an apartment in a gang-controlled territory in Los Angeles, where she saw two separate shootings. She described one incident as follows: "Three guys just went up to a kid and shot him in the head three times." Patti, who had previously lived in the south side of Chicago, stated that she had had "some near misses when gun shots went off" during drive by-shootings in her neighbourhood. When Chira's family left Arizona for Los Angeles, they moved into what she described as "the projects," where gun fights became a normal occurrence. Tiffany had lived most of her adult life in and around the south side of Chicago, when asked if she had ever been exposed to gang-related violence, she replied, "Yeah, several times." After coming home from prison, she noted that the violence had "kinda slowed down, but certain areas still has that gang-related mentality. Back then it was real heavy. You went in the wrong neighbourhood or you said the wrong thing or they wanted to take your shoes or your jacket."

Conclusions

We began this chapter by describing the victimization history of Gillian, a woman who was threatened and abused by her ex-husband, became homeless, and did what she thought was necessary to survive on the streets only to suffer further violence. Gillian's experiences, unfortunately, are all too common for homeless women: violence can often begin a hopeless cycle, leading to homelessness, which, in turn, can increase individual risk of further victimization. Thus, not surprisingly, several of the women in this study, were locked in cycles of both repeat victimization and homelessness.

Violence is a public health issue. In the United States, it has been recognized as such since the late 1970s, as exemplified by the establishment of the Centers for Disease Control's Violence Epidemiology Branch in 1983 (Dahlberg and Mercy 2009). Despite an increasing federal- and state-level focus on violence prevention programs since the 1990s, violence in the U.S. remains a significant problem (FBI 2016) and is a primary cause of both homelessness and poly-homelessness among women (Cooke 2015; Williams 2016). Further, recognition of the detrimental health, social, economic, and other impacts of violence has failed to translate into sufficient public resources for victims of violence, a problem that is particularly acute for homeless women, who lack access to private resources (Huey and Ricciardelli 2016). As a result, many women experience the traumatic effects of victimization on their own. It is this topic – the impact of victimization on homeless women – to which we turn in the next chapter.

Chapter Three

The After-effects of Violence

Now depression, I suffer with badly because ... after my twins' father beat me so bad in 2008, I tried to commit suicide. My children were taken from me as a result of that. They are still in foster care right now, because I'm still suffering from depression and my drug addiction.

– Marlys

Marlys's history of victimization began in childhood. Now forty-four years old, she described a childhood home in which she experienced emotional, mental, and physical abuse at the hands of her mother and stepfather. Then, in her twenties, Marlys met the man who fathered her two children. She stayed in a relationship with him for eight years. Of this relationship, Marlys noted, "He beat me for the whole time."

Marlys is keenly aware of the fact that her experiences of interpersonal violence have produced significant traumatic effects, with which she continues to struggle. Among these effects is a severe, chronic depression that is frequently triggered by exposure to particular sights and sounds. Marlys explained:

Even watching TV shows or movies, when I see that on the TV, it all just comes flooding back. Then, that's where, sometimes, my depression will set back in, especially if I'm by myself. When it hits me, I just close up. I'm like a turtle that sticks his head back in his shell. I just hide.

Bouts of severe depression have led Marlys to try to take her own life. The first attempt occurred in 2008. Since then, Marlys has tried to take her life on two further occasions: once taking a deliberate overdose of pills; another time using a gas oven. When asked what prompted these attempts, Marlys acknowledged they were triggered by painful memories and feelings linked to "my childhood [and being] beaten from my twins' father." Now sober, Marlys admits that she had also tried to deal with her feelings of guilt and shame through the numbing effects of cocaine and alcohol, a response that is not unusual when memories, emotions, and physiological responses arising from violent experiences become overwhelming (Stenius and Veysey 2005).

In this chapter, we examine the after-effects of violent victimization and the ways in which these effects can manifest in the lives of homeless women. We do so by starting from the position advanced by Stenius and Veysey (2005, 1155) that "the violence that women experience has profound effects." Building on this position, we explore how female victims of violence understood the impact of violent victimization on their own lives – that is, as emotional scars; shame; guilt, self-blame, or addiction; cycles of homelessness; and depression, anxiety, and PTSD. Where relevant, we also draw on the literature as it relates to the manifestation of these effects in the lives of both homeless women and among other segments of the population. What doing so reveals is that the prevalence of PTSD, depression, and other negative impacts of violence are typically highest among individuals like those we studied – that is, for marginalized women violence imposes a fairly significant burden, and one that is frequently borne without strong social or therapeutic supports (Huey et al. 2014; Huey and Ricciardelli 2016).

Emotional Impacts

A predominant theme that emerged in women's stories of dealing with violence was the concept of "emotional damage." Most of the women saw themselves as somehow damaged by their experiences and carrying emotional and mental burdens as a result. Leslie had been in an abusive relationship and spoke to the nature of the "damage" she felt she was still carrying in the form of mental and emotional wounds that remained unhealed:

> I do think that domestic violence is a big one because those scars are … they don't heal with physical remedies. It's really, really hard to get down to what's hurting you, emotionally. Like I said earlier, I can think that my issues are related to jobs, money, and homes, but guess what? I still have this huge, traumatic thing that happened to me, that has scarred me emotionally. I'm going to have to deal with that once normalcy comes

back to my life ... I could start dating someone, or I could have a certain co-worker who reminds me of that person. I might feel the same
way I felt when I was in my abusive relationship. I think that when it
comes to emotional scars, they are much harder to put your finger on and
express ... I am very aware that these emotional scars can come up and
be very sabotaging.

Michaele also invoked the metaphor of injury to describe psychological and emotional damage sustained through emotional and physical
abuse she experienced as a child. When asked about the effects of that
abuse, Michaele saw her "emotional injuries" as the worst effects, "'cuz
the scars will heal, but those words, they always linger." Carmela, a
victim of multiple sexual assaults, says of herself, "I'm hurting."
Some women expressed the pain of emotional scars as an onslaught
of sudden feelings that could be triggered by different people and
events. Survivors of trauma often describe external triggers (e.g.,
sights, sounds, smells, or locations) or internal cues (e.g., emotions or
thoughts), or both, that can provoke a flood of painful memories (Joseph
2011). Among our participants, Holly was one of several women who
provided an example of what it felt like when memories of violence
were triggered: "My body wants to cry sometimes. I feel a thick chunk
in my throat and I want to cry." In those moments, "I don't know who
I am." Jamie, who had been sexually assaulted multiple times since she
had become homeless, acknowledged that while she tries to push the
resulting feelings down, "eventually it will bubble up." She described
how this happens: "I've had my moments where it'll be something stupid that happens and I'll start getting really pissed off or I'll start crying
about something little that happens." Ruby, a sixty-year-old IPV survivor, stated that sometimes she would be overwhelmed by her feelings:
"It would just hit me. I didn't care where I was. I would be so upset
and embarrassed. I didn't want to cry out in public, but it was just too
much. Waiting at the train or bus stop, it would just happen." Eve was
unable to even begin the process of discussing the damage inflicted on
her psyche after years of violent victimization. When asked whether
she could talk with a therapist about the damage she carries with her,
she shook her head "no" and started to cry. "I never talk," she whis-
pered. "My past life ... [stops speaking]." Holly described herself as "a
dressed-up garbage can" – that is, as someone whose exterior belies the
inner turmoil she experiences. As Holly explained, "I still have things
I'm working on, I still have feelings."

Another way in which women referenced the emotional impact of violent victimization was through use of the terms "consumed" or "burden to carry." For example, Helen had experienced what she described as "a lot of sexual abuse as a child, domestic violence as an adult." Of these experiences, she said that the most damaging to her was the sexual abuse: "I'm still dealing with it ... I still get a little emotional about it ... It used to eat me up, really, really bad." Alisa was also a victim of sexual abuse. Of the effects of the abuse, she said, "I've been carrying this my whole life. I've never been able to talk to nobody about it. It's been hurting me so much [in] my soul." She also described the memories of the abuse as "haunting" and "terrifying."

Negative Thoughts and Cognitions

Victimization has been linked with distorted beliefs about the self, others, and the world. For example, victims of violence may blame themselves for being attacked and, as a result, may experience feelings of low self-esteem, helplessness, and fear (Janoff-Bulman 1992). Victims of sexual violence are especially likely to express shame (Brown, Testa, and Messman-Moore 2009; Vidal and Petrak 2007; Weiss 2010); confusion, guilt, and anger (Brown, Testa, and Messman-Moore 2009); and feel dehumanized and humiliated (Ullman 1996).

Weiss (2010) has argued that women's shame-based self-narratives are often structured by normative expectations about women's behaviour that differentiate "good girls" from those who get raped. It is, after all, not uncommon to hear suggestions that if a victim had been "acting appropriately" (e.g., wearing conservative clothing, not being in a "dangerous" place, or not consuming alcohol or drugs) she would not have been sexually assaulted. Narratives of self-blame such as those described by Weiss are readily apparent in several statements made by our participants. Many of these women described the after-effects of violence in the form of negative thoughts that frequently led to negative emotions. These negative cognitions principally took two forms: first, as expressions of self-blame regarding the conditions surrounding episodes of violence, and second, as shame over perceived dysfunctions with respect to her ability to cope with the aftermath of that violence. Negative thinking patterns led to feelings of shame and guilt, which, in turn, lowered women's self-esteem. For some participants, those who did not self-describe as "strong," these perceptions caused them to believe they would never recover from violence and possibly never "be normal"; thus, they felt they would be perpetually "weak" and "vulnerable."

This phenomenon was similarly noted in analysing the stories of women who were sexually assaulted as children or adults. Tory, who had an extensive history of physical and sexual victimization beginning in childhood, was sexually assaulted as an adult while under the influence of drugs. Because she was intoxicated at the time, she blamed herself for the assault: "I just think, if you wasn't high, you wouldn't have got raped." Meda, who was sexually assaulted by a male acquaintance while she was drinking, not only struggled with self-blame over the circumstances of her victimization but also had to contend with an unsupportive husband. Her husband, not unlike many other partners of sexual assault victims (Christiansen, Bak, and Elklit 2012), blamed her for the assault, she said, "because he says I shouldn't have been there." As a result, if Meda's husband becomes angry with her, "he just starts flinging off at the mouth" at what he perceives to be her responsibility for her victimization.

It was also not uncommon for women who had been sexually abused as children to assume responsibility for their victimization or for what they saw as maladaptive behaviours they may have subsequently engaged in as a result (see also Barker-Collo 2001). Leslie was molested as a child and consequently began to act out sexually at an early age. Describing how she felt for years following her abuse, she said, "I felt so much shame inside." For years, Sue blamed her body and its early maturation for sexual abuse that occurred within her family: "All the time I was thinking it was because I had big breasts." With the help of a therapist, Sue had only recently begun to challenge this belief. Pamela had been sexually abused by an older brother. Because she had rationalized the experience as "incest," she had been "really ashamed about it for a long time."

Women also tended to blame themselves for the exposure to violence as a result of what several described as poor choices on their part. Sylvie was one. She had witnessed a robbery in a crack house and described both the experience and her subsequent feelings about it:

> I was like, "How could they miss me?" I was on the sofa, covers over my head and everybody's on the floor and I can hear them talking what they was gonna do to these people. But what if it was me? I didn't say anything. It lasted for like five minutes. After they left, I just got up and was overwhelmed. Like I said, this is one of the bad decisions that I made, to be

homeless, because I didn't have to be homeless. I made a bad decision ... it's still in my head today ... You don't have to be homeless if you don't want to. You really don't. You could make better decisions.

Bianca saw herself as making a "poor choice" when she decided to fight back against an ex-boyfriend who she said "hit me": "I tried to fight my way through and ended up hurting my own self. He hurt me and I hurt my own self, too. I put the blame mostly on him, but for me ... doing stupid things and the wrong move? I could've done something else." When asked if she had sought medical help afterwards, she replied, "I just sat there and didn't go that time." Gillian, whose story is partially told in the introduction to the previous chapter, also blamed herself for her victimization: "All these things, I put myself in a way. I was doing drugs, on the street prostituting. I can't blame that on anybody else. I can't if I really want to be realistic about it."

Victims of other non-sexual forms of violence also expressed a significant degree of shame over what had happened to them. Such thinking was particularly notable among victims of IPV. For example, when discussing whether Jodie had ever reported her physical abuse to police or medical professionals, she said no, because "it's a shameful thing that happened ... my husband hit me." When Stephanie was asked if she would ever be willing to participate in group therapy for victims of violence, she responded, "I would get ... I ... I was embarrassed. You know, I'm still ... I'm still ashamed and embarrassed of my situation."

Shame was also present in the words of many participants in relation to what they perceived to be their inability to cope in healthy, constructive ways following a violent experience. Virginia, a forty-five-year-old domestic violence survivor from Detroit, advised that, even in therapeutic settings, she never speaks of either her experiences of abuse or its consequences, which led to a drug addiction that cost her her job and the custody of her children: "For me to sit in a group of people and say, 'I was a battered woman,' or 'I lost my kids in foster care,' or 'I was a drug addict ... I lost my job because I got high on the job,' that's shame." Toni had been physically abused by an ex-partner, as well as sexually assaulted. She subsequently fell apart emotionally and lost custody of her children. Not only did Toni adopt responsibility for the abusive relationship, seeing it as a bad "choice" she had made, but she also carried with her shame and guilt over the loss of her children: "I can blame myself as an adult ... as an adult you have to take responsibilities for your own actions." Benita had struggled for years with depression and addiction following episodes of both intimate partner violence and sexual assault. At one point in her life, she had been hospitalized following a suicide attempt. Through careful questioning it was revealed that she felt ashamed of her perceived inability to cope following the assaults. When asked, "Before you came in here, all of the things that we're talking about, did you feel that it was something to be ashamed of, something strange or abnormal?" she replied, "Yeah." Sondra, who had entered a deep depression from which she was only recently emerging, blamed herself for her perceived inability to cope with decades of violence. Talking about how the depression resulted in periods during which she felt she couldn't be fully present for her children, she said, "I have a lot of guilt."

Shame, guilt, and blame play a role in individuals constructing negative self-appraisals and in lowering self-esteem (Valerio and Lepper 2009). Leslie, who had struggled with shame over her early sexualization following incidents of molestation, admitted that she "felt so crappy about [herself]" and struggled with "poor self-esteem." One of the ways in which these feelings manifest is through overly critical self-appraisals of how she presents herself in the world. "The way I dress," she said, is in clothes she views as "too short" and "too tight." Sue also admitted to struggling with self-esteem issues. Believing that her abuse was the result of early physical maturation, she said of herself, "I wanted to turn into this fat, ugly woman that nobody would like … and I did." As Camelia pointed out, impoverished women who are already experiencing feelings of inadequacy and/or "otherness," also carry the burden of a stigmatized identity: "When you're homeless, you're pushing a shopping cart around, digging through trash cans … you don't feel good enough."

Depression

Rates of diagnosed depression are high within homeless communities, but research suggests that it is still likely underdiagnosed and, thus, undertreated (Huey et al. 2014). To gain insight into the extent to which the women were grappling with post-traumatic effects, interview questions were included that asked them, first, if they had ever received a clinical diagnosis of depression, and if so, when. To capture insights from any individuals who *may* have been struggling with undiagnosed depression, we also asked all of them if they were experiencing one or more of several common symptoms drawn from the relevant literature (c.f. Flemke 2009; Lam and Rosenheck 1998; Goodman, Dutton, and Harris 1997; Goodman and Dutton 1996). Questions included whether the women had experienced extended periods during which they had "feelings of sadness," "extreme fatigue and listlessness," "feeling numb," "social isolation," and "difficulties in grooming and other self-care tasks." We also inquired about symptoms that belong to multiple psychiatric diagnoses, such as "suicidality," "self-injurious behaviours," and "sleeping problems."

Jean was among those women who had been diagnosed with depression. Jean had experienced tremendous physical violence throughout her life and had become fearful of therapy and the thought of having to "talk about the things that took place in your life." Thus, she had only recently been diagnosed with clinical depression following a suicide attempt. Amina was referred to a counselling service by shelter workers, who recognized that she was "very depressed." A survivor of both child abuse and IPV, Amina said that her depression stemmed from holding "everything inside of me to the point where I had a nervous breakdown." What she was holding in, she explained, was "all of this frustration and all of this pain" over what she had experienced. Arlene, who was feeling more emotionally stable at the time of her interview, had spent years living with an abusive husband and had been hospitalized for severe depression after that relationship ended. Of this time in her life she said, "I didn't care about living any more ... I was dirty, I stunk, I never got out of bed." Kat had only recently entered counselling as a result of her ongoing struggles with depression. Having been physically and sexually abused as a child and sexually assaulted as an adult, Kat had made several attempts on her own to "try and let some of it go." However, whenever she thought that she had moved forward, "it comes back to the mind." Describing what happens next, she said, "One minute you're not depressed, and the next minute you're like, 'I can't even get up to take a bath.' That's how depressed I am." For Ruby, who had also spent years in an abusive relationship, depression wasn't isolated to specific times in her life, but was a chronic state that produced feelings that would overwhelm her:

> Anxiety, I think I have conquered anxiety, a long time ago. But, sadness, hurt and feeling alone, I've felt alone my whole life. I would just cry. It would just hit me. I don't care where I was. I would be so upset and embarrassed ... I didn't want to cry out in public, but it was just too much. Waiting at the train or bus stop ... it would just happen.

Anxiety

Like depression, rates of anxiety are believed to be significantly higher among homeless citizens than within the general population (Holt, Montesinos, and Christensen 2007). Therefore, our interview guide also focused on both diagnoses of anxiety-related disorders, as well as typical symptoms associated with anxiety. In relation to the latter, we asked questions about whether women had experienced feelings of "overwhelming fear or dread," "obsessive negative thoughts," or somatic symptoms such as "heart racing" or "panic attacks" (Flemke 2009; Lam and Rosenheck 1998; Goodman, Dutton, and Harris 1997; Goodman and Dutton 1996).

Seven, who at the age of nineteen has been a victim of both physical and sexual assaults, reported several symptoms associated with anxiety, including panic attacks. One of Seven's panic attacks was so severe that it resulted in emergency treatment. Jean had also recently had a panic attack, brought on by her fears of therapy and her concerns about having to disclose decades of physical and sexual assaults. She had decided to begin therapy following a suicide attempt; however, the simple act of setting up the appointment brought on panic: "I had to call the office. There's a woman I talked to and I told her, 'I'm really scared to leave the house. I'm having a panic attack.'" Although never diagnosed as having an anxiety disorder, Tonya had been experiencing panic attacks triggered by frequent worrying, anger, and upset. When asked whether she finds her mind running with obsessive negative thoughts, she admitted, "I constantly does that." Her worrying, she said, would cause her to "get so angry ... I just get sweaty and dizzy. I make myself sick." Recently, she began having panic attacks in other situations, such as when she went to a local thrift store: "When I walked in there, I just started sweating. I still don't know what happened to me. I got real warm. I mean sweat that I could actually wipe off. I got so weak that I just sat down."

Open-ended questions also yielded discussions of other signs of anxiety frequently associated with victimization. For example, Seven has become hypervigilant in social settings: "I don't like to be in small rooms. If you see me, I'm looking at the doors. I don't like to sit with my back turned. I want to be against the wall, so nobody can [sneak up on me]." Mariah, who was jumped by a gang, noted that she could no longer be in a "crowded place" because "I get a headache because you never know what can happen." When Marion was asked if she ever convinces herself that the fears she incessantly worries over are real, she nodded and replied, "[That's] me," before acknowledging that when in this state, she finds herself growing more and more anxious and thus breaking out into a sweat ("a lot"). Tiffany's anxiety manifests in spaces where she feels confined or crowded: "I don't like to be closed in either. People standing in line, all bunched up. Give me some space!"

PTSD

Given the extent to which women in this book had experienced not only violence but also other forms of trauma, it is hardly surprising to note that diagnoses of PTSD were particularly prevalent among the women interviewed. Whereas many of the women interviewed who exhibit symptoms of anxiety and depression remain clinically undiagnosed, all of the women who stated they had PTSD had been clinically diagnosed. Once the diagnosis was discussed, we then asked about specific symptoms they were experiencing.

According to estimates from the Diagnostic and Statistical Manual of Mental Disorders (DSM-5; APA 2013), these lifetime prevalence rate of PTSD is about 9 per cent and the twelve-month prevalence rate is about 3.5 per cent; thus, PTSD is a relatively common diagnosis, although much rarer than other illnesses like depression and anxiety. Still, reported rates of PTSD among homeless women are considerably greater with some suggesting lifetime prevalence rates approaching 35 per cent to 50 per cent (North and Smith 1992; Whitbeck 2009; Whitbeck, Armenta, and Gentzler 2015). Further, as many as one-third of homeless women meet the past-year criteria for PTSD (Whitbeck, Armenta, and Gentzler 2015). Victimization has been found to significantly predict PTSD among homeless women (Whitbeck, Armenta, and Gentzler 2015).

Of the nine different types of violence women in our samples stated they had experienced, only one woman – Julia, who grew up in a gang-associated family, spent years living off the street and in and out of crack houses, and who still maintained active gang relations – reported experiencing all nine. As one might expect, Julia, who acknowledged that sometimes she gets "broke down," has been diagnosed with PTSD. Sharleen has also been diagnosed with PTSD: "I'm post-traumatic stress due to the rape." In discussing her diagnosis, Josie pointed to her early life explaining, "I had some very traumatic experiences during my childhood with emotional and psychological abuse, physical abuse and stuff." When asked if she felt that memories of that abuse some-times surfaced in unexpected ways, she acknowledged experiencing post-traumatic flashbacks, particularly "when someone asks me about it." As a result of these flashbacks, "that led me to be diagnosed with PTSD." Nadia had also been diagnosed with PTSD and clinical depres-sion because, as she explained, "I've been raped multiple times. I've been beaten multiple times." She also suffers panic attacks. During one three-day period, she had "seven of them and I couldn't stop it." For Leslie, who has also been diagnosed with PTSD, the world is "frighten-ing as hell. Going out in the world, communicating, all of it ... it's all very exhausting [*laughs*]."

Addiction

Several of the women reported past or present addictions to drugs or alcohol. This is not surprising given that the link between traumatic experience and alcohol and drug use as coping mechanisms are well-known (Beckham et al. 1995; Kilpatrick et al. 1997; Salomon, Bassuk, and Huntington 2002), and that there are high rates of both victimiza-tion and these forms of "self-medication" (Cappell and Greeley 1987), or "chemical avoidance" (Briere 1989), within homeless populations (Upshur, Weinreb, and Bharel 2014).

Carmela was one of the women who linked her addiction to early experiences of violence, which included growing up in a physically abusive environment. Describing her childhood as "heavy stuff, noth-ing was beautiful," she felt that she had "had to be grown up." As an adult, she had consciously or otherwise reverted back to childhood: "I feel like I'm a child now." However, the aspect of childhood that she openly acknowledged clinging to was a desire not to be responsible: "I procrastinate on everything in life but the dope." Pamela had grown up in a family in which her father was physically abusive to her mother. As a young adult, she entered into her own abusive relationship: "I thought it was okay. For a long period of time I let him hit me and slap me around." To cope with the abuse, she turned to "shooting up coke, shooting up heroin, pills, methadone, drinking, just about everything."

Rather than seeing her addictions as a direct consequence of a vio-lence-filled childhood, Blue blamed herself for not only her mother's death but also for her drug use turning into a full-blown addiction. As a child, Blue had grown up in an extremely abusive environment. By the time she had left home at the age of fifteen to run to the streets, she had been physically and sexually abused and observed multiple episodes of violence. During this time, she admitted, she "got involved with a lot of things – prostitution, selling drugs, and using drugs." Blue attributes her addiction not to her experiences of abuse but to the death of her mother. Blue's mother had been shot and killed by an unknown assailant who broke into the woman's home. "I was addicted to alcohol, cocaine, marijuana," she advised. "I used drugs because I thought my mother's death was my fault because the things I was doing on the streets."

Multiple Episodes of Homelessness

Among the after-effects of violence, one that has received insufficient attention is experiences of multiple episodes of homelessness – that is, violent victimization as a potential causal factor in women experiencing multiple episodes of homelessness (Broll and Huey forthcoming). Of our 187 participants, nearly half (43 per cent) reported experiencing more than one episode of homelessness in their lives. Sue's story represents a case in point.

Sue first became homeless at the age of thirteen. Her homelessness was precipitated by sexual abuse, first, by her stepfather and then, when she went to live with him, by her father. Now thirty-six years old, Sue has never had a stable home, bouncing instead from the streets to hotels to shelter beds. Sexually abused as a child, Charlie had a similar history, one that also included episodes of acting out that led to stints in juvenile hall. As a teenager and young adult, she was "hanging out with a motorcycle club … [and] at that time that was my home." After having experienced multiple episodes of homelessness over the years, accompanied by experiences of physical, sexual, and intimate partner violence, at age fifty-eight Charlie had been most recently homeless for five years. Andrea was also sexually abused as a child, which led to her early departure from home. At first, she simply "went to family's houses," before turning to the streets at age thirteen. Now thirty-eight years old, Andrea's most recent stint of shelter residency, some three months, represents what she describes as the "the longest that I've been in a shelter, off the street."

Whereas many of the women's stories of living through multiple episodes of homelessness began in adolescence, some women, like Renisa, first became homeless as adults. Renisa, who described herself as homeless "off and on for years," said of herself that the "first time I was homeless I was in an abuse situation ... [and] it just spiralled from there." She further explained, "Once you become a battered person, it's likely you'll be homeless every year." In her own case, she said, "it seems like every other year, I just can't get it together."

Conclusions

Marlys's experiences are fairly representative of the long-term conse-quences of violence described by the women interviewed. Some women described their "emotional scars" as long-lasting and persistent, accom-panied by powerful emotions that could be triggered by events, people, or circumstances. As we noted earlier, these feelings are not unique to this cluster of women: homeless women experience a much higher rate of PTSD than the general population (North and Smith 1992; Whitbeck 2009; Whitbeck, Armenta, and Gentzler 2015). Other traumatic effects post-violent victimization documented include depression and anxiety, as well as addictions to drugs and alcohol. We also note that violence and other traumas in their life histories led to multiple experiences of homelessness for a number of the women.

In addition to formal mental health diagnoses and disorders, victimi-zation distorted many women's beliefs about themselves and others. As others have found, our participants experienced feelings of shame and self-doubt after being victimized. The women often blamed themselves for being physically or sexually assaulted, suggesting that they drank too much, wore clothes that were too revealing, or should have known better than to be in a particular place at a specific time. Sometimes, the families of survivors also blamed the women for being assaulted. Combined, these feelings lowered women's self-esteem and produced negative self-appraisals.

Since we also know that important barriers to service exist for home-less women (Huey, Fthenos, and Hryniewicz 2012; Gelberg et al. 2004; Halton 1997; Heslin, Andersen, and Gelberg. 2003; Jasinski et al. 2010; Mikhail and Curry 1999; Stermac and Paradis 2001), what can be done? How can homeless women – many of whom do not have the ability to seek out, attend, or pay for counselling and other healthcare services – overcome the effects of violent victimization? In the next chapter, we examine some of the internal and external resources women draw upon in order to cope with violence and its aftermath and, in some cases, to even develop resilience and enjoy personal growth.

Chapter Four

The Process

It's never an overnight thing, [it takes] baby steps.

– Chrissie

Chrissie has been homeless multiple times over the past forty-two years. The story of her homelessness begins in childhood. Her father raised her until she was nine years old. At age nine, social services removed Chrissie from her father's care and placed her into the foster care system until she turned eighteen. Of her mother, Chrissie says, she "was never around," and "was a whore," so Chrissie doesn't "trust women for shit." After becoming a ward of the state, Chrissie's life did not improve. As a teenager, Chrissie was sexually assaulted twice and found herself in a series of physically abusive relationships. As an adult, she developed an addiction to crystal methamphetamine ("meth") and spent years alternating between holding employment, losing work, staying at motels, and sleeping on the streets.

Chrissie, who has been diagnosed as having PTSD, bipolar disorder, and attention deficit hyperactivity disorder (ADHD), is keenly aware of the fact that she carries with her deep emotional scars, and she willingly acknowledged that the idea of probing them through therapy invokes fear: "I'm not comfortable with them getting too far deep into me. It's terrifying for anybody." Although she wants to move past her issues, and is attending couple's therapy, she is "not really happy" with her life and worries that opening up about her past will push her into a major depressive episode at a time when she is just starting to get back on her feet: "I have a job, I have [a partner]." Like many of the women interviewed, Chrissie has been working on addressing some of her issues on her own by using various coping strategies, particularly mental strategies that included trying to change her "self-talk." As she noted, her efforts often produced mixed results: "Until you change the way you think, you're not going to change the way you are, so I try to think differently about my depression, but there is just times it's too overwhelming. I can't do it."

The central message of Chrissie's story – that recovery from violence, often from a lifetime of violence, is a process, and not a simple one at that – is visible in comments she made at the end of her interview when discussing her own experiences with psychotherapy:

> The way I look at it is, ask any psychiatrist, anything you have issues with or distrust or whatever, all stems from your childhood. It all has roots from your childhood … something that is very important to know about a person is why they are the way they are today, because then you get a better chance of understanding who they are and figuring out different ways of handling them. But some people are just not willing do to that and are not ready for it.

Although Chrissie is open to change, and has been developing her own insights into her life, she is also admittedly one of those women who is, at this point in her life, "not ready" for the deep psychological work necessary to begin shifting the weight of years of violence, emotional and financial deprivation, interpersonal betrayals, and other traumas. It is not that Chrissie is stuck, mentally or otherwise; rather, to protect herself psychologically, she needs to take "baby steps" and requires tremendous support to even begin these small steps.

It has been suggested that homeless women, in general, may be uniquely resilient given the combined hardships they face (Cohen 2001). While we would not go that far in our claims, we do agree that many of the individuals we interviewed did exhibit a remarkable degree of willingness to overcome violence and current adversity (principally homelessness), and most were taking steps to deal with their victimization history, homelessness, or both. This is not to say that the majority had successfully overcome either, but rather that most were engaged in the process.

In the pages that follow we link elements of the resilience literature to women's narratives to explore the process by which they attempt to, or in some cases, achieve resilience. In particular, we draw on four key concepts that help us to illustrate this process: "moving on," "active healing," "goal setting," and "closure." These concepts, and our use of them, will be explained in further detail in each section. We also include what we see as a useful fifth concept: being "stuck."

"Moving On" as an Attitude

In discussing the process of becoming resilient, our participants most frequently used phrases that involved movement, such as "moving on," "moving it," and "moving forward." For example, in discussing why Helen believes that it is important for her to talk about victimization in her past, she informed us, "It's not mine, so you can have it." This was a coping strategy she had learned – "grew into" through therapy, she said – and was exemplified best by the phrase, "Put it out there and move on." Moving on is not simply an act, or a movement in the process, but rather signals the start of a shift in attitude, which typically includes acceptance of what has happened and a commitment to some form of positive change, as defined by the individual (Richmond et al. 2000). In relation to addressing the aftermath of violence, some have described moving on in the following terms: "[It] entails no longer being confined by a survivor identity but being free to construct a life that has meaning beyond the past and its overwhelming definition of self as someone who is circumscribed by the experience" (Jones 2007, 150).

Blue was among those women who were in the early stages of coming to terms with her experiences of violence. She saw herself as ready to move forward in life, and was, for the first time, willing to go into therapy. However, she remained fearful of therapy and the emotions it might dredge up. Regarding therapy, she said, "I would like to get [it], giving me the knowledge to better myself, giving me encouragement." Yet she worried that she would be forced to relive her mother's death, which would "put me back into depression." Marlys had yet to let go of painful memories of her abusive mother, now deceased: "Constantly reliving it, you'll never get over it ... You need to move past it ... My mother has been dead for fifteen years ... It was a relief ... I was really struggling with how to let her rest in peace, because she did me so wrong." Unlike Blue, Marlys had already begun therapy and was working on finding a way to resolve her feelings towards her mother in a way that would bring a form of empathetic closure. Marlys said, "After talking to my therapist about things that she [her mother] was probably going through, in her life, that she was struggling with ... she never talked to anybody about

what she was going through ... she wanted to be that strong figure."
Speaking of her history of childhood physical and sexual abuse, Barb
stated she had also sought counselling, in order to "move it," meaning the mental and emotional burden that that abuse had placed upon
her. She acknowledged that "it's not easy" to just "move it," but that
she was able to see that her past had given her both "advantages and
its disadvantages." Among those advantages, Barb cited, was the
ability to survive and overcome obstacles: "You're not gonna shoot
me down. I'm a fighter. I hear negativity, 'You can't do this,' and I'll
try to prove them wrong."

Many women also recognized that "moving on" was not a straight-
forward exercise, but a struggle in which one faces challenges, roadblocks, and even setbacks. Toni's comments illustrate this best. When
asked if she was in the "process of dealing," she replied, "I try to be,
but when you look at reality ... you want to be real ... you try to be
optimistic and there's a lot of quotes for that ... But the real-world
challenges that, so I'm trying." Caprice shared a similar outlook: "I
do what I have to do. I stay focused ... and yeah, it gets hard. You cry
at times, but you wipe your eyes and move on." Forty-five-year-old
Tracy had experienced a lifetime of physical and sexual assaults and,
for her, moving on was something she had at least partially achieved:
"I think I've sort of let go of the past. I try to forgive, so that I can move
on with things."

Some of the women employed different metaphors for explaining
where they were in relation to the process of "moving on" from residual
emotional pain. Like Barb, Meri employed fighting imagery. "You fight
back and become something. You fight back and you stand up." Sylvie,
who saw her victimization as a consequence of "bad choices in my life,"
decided that if she had chosen to be in harmful situations, she could
also exercise agency to make different choices. Thus, for Sylvie, moving on was about correcting her perceived mistakes of the past: "I'm
going to correct my bad decision to a positive decision." Seeing her life
this way, although in one sense reaffirming the self-blaming that leads
to shame and guilt, allowed Sylvie to feel autonomous in a situation –
living within a shelter – in which most women feel highly dependent
and vulnerable. It also provided Sylvie with the hopeful belief that she
could move on from the past by trying to "better myself." For Anisha,
"moving on" is about "being open" about who one is and what one
wants from life, which includes being open to discussing one's experiences. She explained:

I see a lot of men and women they haven't dealt with it [violence] ... so
they hide it away. Maybe if they would've dealt with it, their lives would
be so much better. I find myself very open. I find myself very intelligent.
I find myself wanting a good life, but I never worked for it. I don't feel
like I've changed as a person. I'm still the same person. But when I was in
rehab, it was an opening to me ... I was just completely open.

Rosa used the phrases "getting over it" and "leaving it behind" to
describe both her personal goal of overcoming violence and where she
was in that process. "I'm trying to get over it now," she said. "I can't get
over what happened to me when I was young, but I'm ready to start
leaving it behind me."

Active Healing

Whereas "moving on" is an attitude shift, "active healing" is the steps
taken to manifest that shift, whether that be in the form of conscious
changes to one's mindset or beliefs or physical changes to enhance
one's well-being and growth (Bogar and Hulse-Killacky 2006). Active
healing can take many forms, but our participants most frequently referenced two: taking responsibility for one's own recovery and rejecting
the role of victim (see also Stenius and Veysey 2005; Bogar and Hulse-
Killacky 2006).

Sylvie is trying to move forward – to "better myself," as she said –
by taking responsibility for her own recovery from violence. To that
end, she had left the Chicago streets to enter a shelter, where she was
actively engaged in numerous housing, employment, and counselling
programs. When Marion was asked about her willingness to attend
counselling services to deal with the trauma from physical abuse that
began in childhood and continued through adulthood, she stated that
she would gratefully accept any assistance she could receive: "Everything that they can offer me, I need the help."

Unfortunately, many of the women were residing in facilities that
were unable to provide access to counselling and other healthcare services; others simply failed to ask women about their history of violence
in order to facilitate such access (see also Stenius and Veysey 2005; Huey
et al. 2014). These obstacles did not stop several individuals from seeking out those services themselves, though, in order to advance their
recovery process. As an example, to begin addressing the after-effects
of a sexual assault, Meda, who was in drug and alcohol counselling,

asked her addiction counsellor to help her get into a counselling program that would focus on recovery from violence. She had been experiencing post-traumatic flashbacks and "wanted to understand what was going on with me better." Josie had a history of suicide attempts beginning in childhood. Thus, when she began to experience suicidal feelings again, she decided that she was "not doing the right thing" and also sought out therapeutic services on her own. Although Frida was not currently in therapy, she was actively looking for counselling or a therapeutic program. "I have to have treatment," she said. "I think it's child abuse ... I do not know. For a year and a half. To try and get me flashbacks and nightmares." When asked what she sought from therapy, she replied, "To better myself. To move on."

Identifying as victims made many women feel weak, passive, or vulnerable. In order to move on, it was necessary for these individuals to reject the role of victim, and to see themselves as someone who went through an ordeal and has instead emerged from it stronger and not defined by it (see Jones 2007). As Mariah explained, "When you go through stuff like that, it makes you a better and stronger person." Mariah felt that instead of identifying as a victim, and being seen by others as one, it was preferable to "have 'I am me' on your shoulder and 'this made me a stronger person.'" For her, rejecting the role of victim would allow her to reverse a perceived dichotomy between victim/weak and offender/strong: "The person that did it to you is going to become a weak person." Candy similarly believed it was necessary to acknowledge being victimized but to avoid adopting the role of victim because it would become "your crutch for people to feel sorry for you." As she explained, "I was raped and everything. I really have a problem when women hang on to that ... you just have to get over it and move on because it's done, it's over." She felt that adopting "victim" as one's master status – "play yourself as a victim all the time," as she stated it – would mean "that's what's going to happen to you all the time. You're gonna be a victim, over and over and over."

Whereas women like Candy rejected the role of victim because they saw it as an emotional crutch that could keep them trapped in that role (i.e., it would further victimize them), Rosa openly acknowledged that she viewed her victimization as, in her own words, "an excuse" for some of her own behaviours, which included shoplifting and drug use. However, recognizing the need for change, Rosa said of herself that one of those changes was rejecting the victim role: "I've gotten to the point where I don't want to use the past and everything that happened in my past to act the way I do now. It's getting kind of old. I'm thirty-two years old and I'm making excuses as to why I act the way I act because of what happened to me when I was 8, 9, 10, 11, 12. That excuse is getting old." Now in therapy, Rosa also rejected her therapist's attempts at explaining current problem behaviours as products of the past:

He's like, "You acted like this because look what happened in your past." I was like, "Can we not talk about my past? I'm tired of making excuses." I'm this way because of this, because of that … I'm done with all that. My whole life has been revolving around I had a really shitty childhood.

Setting Goals and Having Dreams

Future-oriented thinking is generally characterized as a useful coping strategy for those dealing with unhealed trauma (Bogar and Hulse-Killacky 2006; Park and Slattery 2014). Reassessing one's life goals (Norris 1990) and developing a sense of meaning in life (Park and Slattery 2014) can help survivors overcome traumatic experiences. Through analysis of the interview data it was seen that such thinking – particularly in relation to setting goals or having dreams for one's future – was often an indicator of where women were in relation to the process of recovery. In other words, women who saw themselves as resilient and trying to achieve closure were more likely to talk about the future. In contrast, women who felt weak, vulnerable, and saw themselves as not progressing in their recovery were more past and present-oriented, seldom expressing hopes for the future.[1] A clear example of this is illustrated by Sue, a thirty-six-year-old Los Angeles woman with a history of IPV, childhood sexual abuse, and sexual assaults in adulthood. Sue saw herself as being in the early stages of recovery from the violence in her life. When asked if she was looking forward to her future, she responded, "Now. Before I didn't think about the future. I'm starting to get those feelings." Yvonne described herself as "doing good." Having left two decades of physical abuse (perpetrated by both parents and an abusive partner), she described herself as "just looking forward and just giving it … using my entire life and giving it everything I have."

---

1 Recall from chapter 1 that most of our participants (90 per cent) self-identified as "strong." In contrast, approximately 7 per cent of women described themselves as "weak," and 3 per cent were unsure.

In describing her recovery from an abusive relationship, Michaele similarly said, "Nowadays I try to keep focused on, 'What's my next goal?' I have a lot of goals."

The most common form in which future-oriented thinking was expressed by the women interviewed was through discussions of future professional goals (see also Bogar and Hulse-Killacky 2006). Brittney had both immediate and long-term goals. Of her immediate focus, she stated, "I just want to make money so I can go back to being a productive person." Her longer-term plan was to "go back to school for law and criminal justice." Truly wanted to go back to college to take courses in business and was "trying to get in school ... I want to register in for this semester for fall." Kodi, a writer and natural comedian, was developing a one-woman show that would contain both set pieces and improv. Andrea had moved to Los Angeles to pursue a similar "ultimate dream" of performing comedy.

In many instances women were either beginning along the path towards bringing their goals to fruition or were already well into the process. When Lake was interviewed, she said of herself, "I have major goals," some of which she had already begun pursuing. "Right now, I've just applied for a maternity home. There's a school. I already spoke with the counsellor there and I'm already eligible for their grant. The classes are already paid for ... I'm going to study business administration. I'm excited!" Leslie had left an abusive husband and, in the short term, was "looking for a job and a place to stay." In the meantime, she was "in law school" and continuing her studies while living in shelters across Detroit. Sheran was in school to acquire her GED. In Chicago, twenty-year-old Bianca said of herself, "I'm in college right now, taking general education." Like some of the other women, Bianca's future plans were fairly elaborate, indicating that she had spent a lot of time and effort in thinking through what she wanted for her future. In Bianca's case, she had two goals. The first was to "be a motivational speaker" for "young girls who are having problems," and the second was to develop school-based programming for young women that would "give them a boost up." As an example, she referenced getting youth involved in theatre activities on important issues: "Act it out. Use characters to show people how the dialogue should look like between a guy and girl, for example ... something that helps them learn lessons."

Bianca was not the only woman whose future goals centred on the idea of drawing on her own experiences to help other women and who was taking steps to make those goals a reality. Sometimes, survivors feel called upon to fulfil a mission, which might include helping others who have been similarly victimized, or dedicating themselves to raising public awareness about violence (Herman 1992). Angela had recently gotten her cosmetology license "because my heart is to go to different DV [domestic violence] shelters, rehabs, homeless shelters and do makeovers for the ladies because so many women get stuck in the era before the trauma happened, or they're so scarred on the outside." She further explained, "There were times I saw scars on my face that other people don't see, because I remembered the abuse and I had to work through that." Thus, Angela had developed a plan "to go to the cosmetology schools and get them to help me because it teaches our younger girls how to have compassion and it promotes women-to-women relationships." Sondra, who makes her living selling bottles of water on the streets of Los Angeles, wanted to develop her entrepreneurial skills in order to develop a profitable business. Her long-term dream, though, is to be able to start a non-profit agency to help families of incarcerated loved ones. Referring to the families of inmates, she asked, "Who's gonna teach you how to support them while they're in there? It gets expensive. The phone call. The writing. The packages. The visits. The transportations."

Some women also referenced smaller personal goals that included finding a home and/or mending past relationships. For example, when Ava spoke about her future she stated a goal of "[fixing] my broken family." She also spoke of wanting her own home "to be able to make things like that happen." To illustrate, she added, "My parents had a place where we could come and share Thanksgiving and share a love with each other and we don't have that. That's what's missing. A place to settle, a common ground." Sharleen wanted to "be a better reader." She also wanted to "get custody of my grandson and have me a house." Forty-seven-year-old Ruby was "feeling good" because she was in the process of enacting one of her goals: "I'm looking for my apartment." For Ruby, having her own place was seen as marking "a new chapter in my life."

Closure

One of the key questions asked of study participants was whether they felt they had achieved a sense of "closure" in relation to their experiences of past victimization. Put most simply, "psychological closure is the feeling of completeness of an experience, providing a feeling

4.1. Sondra's business, Los Angeles. Photo: L. Huey, 2013.

of pastness or distance between an experience and the current time" (Namkoong and Gershoff 2012, 690). We use the term to indicate that an individual had processed her experience, come to terms with it both cognitively and emotionally (Beike and Wirth-Beaumont 2005; Beike, Adams, and Wirth-Beaumont 2007), placed it in the past, and was now in a relative state of peace without obvious lingering emotional and mental signs of victimization (Bonugli, Lesser, and Escandon 2013). We asked about the achievement of this state, despite the view, in some quarters, that closure is a "myth" (Boss 2010).

As the responses in the "moving on" section of this chapter indicate, most of the individuals interviewed were still in the process of trying to achieve this state. However, a minority of women (17 per cent) felt they had achieved closure, and it is important to acknowledge that achievement. For Holly, closure came not from the death of an abuser but through a feeling of self-acceptance. "I'm at peace," she said, "I'm okay with myself. I'm no longer ashamed of myself." Referring to herself in the third person, Holly added, "She doesn't do shame, guilt, or resentment on herself anymore."

Acceptance of the past was critical to Jessie's sense of closure related to past experiences of sexual molestation and IPV. "I'm not embarrassed or ashamed by it [being victimized]," she said, "I have nothing to hide." Anisha simply said of the violence in her life, "I finally accepted it and got over it." Seven also felt that she had "accepted it." Referring specifically to her experience of having been sexually exploited by a pimp as a teenager, she said, "I accepted it ... it's in the past. I'm still living, I'm still breathing." Today, she prefers to see this period of her life as "a stepping stone" to better things. Ava, who went from childhood abuse to an abusive relationship as an adult, felt that not only had she achieved closure on the past, but that she had grown as a person. "I'm actually proud of that part of me because I was stagnated for a long time."

As may be recalled from the last chapter, for years Alisa was "haunted" by childhood experiences of sexual and physical abuse. These memories were "very terrifying," she said. When asked about whether she had been able to achieve any sense of closure in relation to that abuse, she replied in the positive. This closure came about as a result of her awareness that her abusers were dead and she felt that she no longer had to live in fear of them: "Now he's dead and I'm kinda glad. I feel kinda better now ... He's gone and I know he can't hurt me no more and my aunt can't hurt me."

Stuck

Whereas the majority of women participating saw themselves as either ready to, or already actively engaged, in some stage of moving past their experiences of violence and its consequences, some women felt "stuck" – that is, they were unable to move forward. For example, Anisha felt that she was going through the motions of life rather than actually living. Only twenty-four years old, and struggling with her experiences of molestations and family dysfunction, she felt that she hadn't "really dealt with life the last ten years."

Like Alisa, Carmela likened the emotional and psychological effects of past abuse to being "haunted" – that is, as a power or force over which she had little control. "Mentally, it's still in mind, the past, they come and haunt me," she said. Robin expressed her perception of her own untreated trauma in similar fashion: "I've witnessed a lot and experienced a lot against me, and other people. I've ... too much. It's all coming back to haunt me now."

Sondra's story underscores the fact that resilience is a process that comes not only with challenges but sometimes with significant setbacks. She was currently stuck, having entered a long period of depression in which she felt unable to cope. Of her past, she simply said, "I couldn't even describe to you some of the things I've seen," before admitting that she was currently "shut down" because she had grown "really tired of being strong." Elaborating on what "shutting down" meant, she described being in "a real bad funk," from which she was only beginning to emerge. The depression had been sufficiently severe that she was unable to "shake it off" to attend her son's graduation. The loss of that experience, on top of everything else she had been through, added a guilt dimensions that "fucked me up really bad," she noted. Tiffany was also openly struggling. She felt that it was her innate nature to be strong, but that her present living situation – a bleak shelter in Chicago that offered little more than warehouse accommodations – was sapping that strength:

> I feel that I'm very strong, especially to deal with the things that go on. I know that here lately, I've been feeling a little weak. Just the littlest things just gets to me and I feel that there's no hope. But at a point in time, I was very strong, that nothing's going to stop me, I'm just gonna keep going. Here lately I've been feeling like I'm not gonna get back down. But I still try and get up and do what I can. Try to stay positive. Things are gonna get better for me.

For some women, the feeling of being stuck was tied to their reliance on drugs or alcohol to help them cope with past trauma and present stressors, which often resulted in a cycle of inertia followed by despair. Jessie saw herself as "choos[ing] not to be sober" but could not articulate reasons for this "choice." The untreated trauma she was struggling with, and her coping strategy of drugs and alcohol, caused her deep unhappiness, but she felt unable to make different "choices": "I started doing other drugs … I don't know why. I don't know what's wrong with me [*crying*]. I feel like I don't even know me anymore." Anisha also used drugs to cope, but had a firmer understanding of the causes of her addiction and the consequences of her usage. She admitted, "I went so long trying to get sober, but not really wanting to." Anisha only went into treatment after losing her home, her job, and nearly her custody of her child. Shania was also stuck and admitted to using substances and social isolation during periods of depression: "I smoke, use drugs, and just pretty much be by myself." Shania did, however, acknowledge that her method "doesn't work" in that "it doesn't relieve the pain and stress away. It just makes it worse." By worse, she further admitted that she was "stuck."

Conclusions

Most of the women discussed in this chapter are, or want to be, on the path to achieving some sense of closure in relation to their victimization, as well as developing a measure of resilience to allow them to overcome present and future difficulties. However, as this chapter also makes evident, this process is neither linear nor easy (Joseph 2011). Some women, like Sondra, can be making progress and then encounter a challenge that saps their "strength," or they may simply find the chronic stressors of everyday life as a victimized homeless woman too big of a drain on their emotional and mental resources. For Tiffany, her bleak living conditions – a gloomy, warehouse-like shelter – caused her to stumble and, at times, feel hopeless, "stuck."

Despite the challenging path to recovery for some of our participants, one constant for several was their optimism and a belief that they would succeed in the face of many obstacles. For example, Toni described how she sometimes takes a moment to herself to cry, but then wipes her eyes and moves on. Words and images like these suggest a hidden resilience that might otherwise seem at odds with their individual surroundings and situations, a topic we will address in greater detail in the next chapter.

Chapter Five

Resilience Determinants

INTERVIEWER: So, you're an optimist?

CHINA: Yeah.

INTERVIEWER: Do you think that plays a role in your being strong?

CHINA: It probably do.

China is a thirty-six-year-old African American woman, who has been staying in a Detroit shelter for a couple of months. Three months prior to entering the shelter, she had been living "down South" with an abusive husband. After fleeing her ex-husband, China moved north and became homeless. Her marriage was only the most recent abusive relationship she had experienced – China grew up in a physically abusive household. She entered her first serious relationship, which lasted for three years, at age eighteen. "It was, like, towards the end [that] he started being abusive," she said. Nine years later China married her now ex-husband who similarly became abusive towards her during the final stages of their relationship.

China has periodically contemplated suicide and was recently diagnosed with depression. Although she has not formally been diagnosed with an anxiety disorder, China reveals that she also experiences some anxiety-like symptoms, such as obsessive worrying, and, when she still lived in the South, somatic symptoms whenever she was anywhere near her former home. The nightmares she used to have about the abuse have now stopped.

When China is asked if she sees herself as "strong," she responds immediately: "I do, considering where I've been and came from, yeah." At first, she credits her strength to the fact she "had, like, strong grandparents" who raised her to also be strong. She then also credits the support of her friends: "I have a friend that's my support system. He gets me through like everything. I have two other ones. They get me through everything that I'm going through. They make me so strong today." Lastly, and only when directly asked, she acknowledges that there is some element of her personality that has also helped her to keep going in the face of both the violence she has endured and its repercussions. For China, that element is optimism: "I see the positive." When asked about her future, China's response illustrates this optimism:

INTERVIEWER: Are you thinking about what you want for your future?
CHINA: My future looks good at this present time in my life.
INTERVIEWER: Which is pretty good considering ...
CHINA: [*Nods*] ... where I came from and my upbringing.

When asked what resources they drew upon to help them in the process of overcoming violence, several women similarly cited an optimistic outlook. Others referred to their determination, their spiritual faith or their ability to connect with others as sources of both comfort and strength. As we noted in the introduction, scholars refer to these characteristics and/or social supports as "resilience determinants" (Connor and Zhang 2006), and they are an important component in helping women to overcome violence (Bonugli, Lesser, and Escandon 2013). In a comparable study of homeless women dealing with both violence and serious mental illness, Bonugli, Lesser, and Escandon observed that "as the women described past traumatic experiences, they revealed personal strengths that carried them through the adversities associated with homelessness, victimization, addictions, and SMI [serious mental illness] and allowed them, once in a safe environment, to move forward" (2013, 832). The women in our sample are dealing with the same issues; however, where they differ is that they had not yet transitioned into stable housing. Yet many were still attempting to "move forward" from violent pasts, a challenge made inordinately more complex without the security of a permanent home. For these women, as we discuss below, personal and social supports are critical factors in both their daily survival and in developing resilience.

Personal Qualities

INTERVIEWER: Where does that strength come from?
BARB: It comes from me, actually.

As can be seen in the interview excerpt above, when Barb, a survivor of childhood abuse, was asked about the source of her "strength," she attributed it to herself, to her own will and determination. The importance of certain personal qualities to both adaptability (in this case the ability to adapt to and survive in the streets) and to the ability to overcome adversity (such as homelessness, violence, loss of children, loss of other family and friends, and so forth), cannot be understated. What might be confused or misunderstood is our use of the term "personal qualities" to describe certain personality components. In this context, we use "personal qualities" to describe a constellation of traits formed through the dynamic interaction of biological bases and social environments (Bandura 1971). As Barb and other women exemplify through their struggles, "strength" can be "learned" as can certain forms of intelligence or "smarts" (like "street smarts"), sociability, adaptability, and other aspects of women's personalities discussed below.

Primary among the personal qualities women cited as key to the process of "moving on" was having a positive outlook and attitude. Perhaps this should be hardly surprising, given that scholars have identified optimism as an important resilience determinant across multiple populations (Bonanno and Keltner 1997; Joseph 2011; Everly, McCormack, and Strouse 2012; Keltner and Bonanno 1997; Taylor et al. 2000; Valentine and Feinauer 1993; Waugh 2014). The intrinsic value of optimism has not always been recognized, though. Indeed, in past years' positivity was thought to be a form of unhealthy denial (e.g., Bowlby 1980). Now, it is recognized as helpful in minimizing the harmful effect of negative cognitions and, therefore, in reducing stress (Keltner and Bonanno 1997), improving the strength of one's social ties (Bonanno and Keltner 1997), and promoting problem solving (Waugh 2014). Optimists also tend to be more task oriented and committed to success than others (Everly, McCormack, and Strouse 2012), and it is believed they tend to exhibit healthier coping strategies (Joseph 2011).

Truly, who had been abused throughout her childhood, attributed her ability to continue surviving and facing chronic adversity to "me." In particular, she felt that she was a positive person and that this quality helped her to keep going. Virginia exemplified this trait when she described how she feels about the shelter environment in which she was living: "I'm a good morning person. I'm not looking at last night. Once the morning starts, it's a new day. So, when I go, 'Good morning!' and you see people, 'What's good about it?' That's depressing. I don't want to function like that." Her positive disposition also manifests in feelings of gratitude, including feeling grateful for having a bed in a Detroit shelter:

> I'm grateful that I woke up this morning and I'm not where I was. I feel like my worries are few, because I woke up this morning and I'm not where I was. I have the lights on, the lights aren't cut off. I'm not getting what I want for breakfast and yet I'm not hungry. I'm grateful.

To illustrate her positive outlook, Ava employed the metaphor of the glass being half full: "I see it like that [at] all times … I feel like a little drop and little drop and a little drop is gonna fill a bucket eventually." Like Virginia, Ava expresses not only hope, but gratitude: "I'm grateful for the little things." Cynthia is another individual with a positive attitude. She too expressed gratitude for her life, despite the challenges that had come with it: "I've had a blessing life, the good and the bad was all my shit. The good has always outweighed the bad for me. As long as I'm breathing, what do I have to complain about?"

In describing themselves as having positive personalities, some of the women referred to themselves specifically as "optimists." Angela said of herself, "I've always been optimistic despite my trials." As a result, and despite the fact that she had been addicted to drugs and relapsed on multiple occasions, "I always had that little glimmer of hope that always got me up and back on track." When Dagmar was asked about whether she saw herself as optimistic, she replied, "Yeah, I think I am … if everything is wrong you have to find the one thread that's okay to hang on to." To illustrate this mental process, she added, "Yeah, I'm homeless, but I'm not in the street. But if you're in the street, you're in the street, but I still have my faculties, I'm still together." Rather than employing the term "optimistic" to describe her outlook, Gillian used the word "hope":

> What is in me? In my heart, there is this hope that no matter what it won't go away. After everything I've been through. All these things – I put myself in a way – I was doing drugs, on the street prostituting … there is just this hope in my heart. Even though there were times it felt like it was gone and other times where it felt like it was dwindling down, it never left me. I always kept my hope for a better future and now the hope in my heart is immense.

Drawing on her positive outlook on life, Ava refashions even her worst experiences into positive steps towards personal growth: "Everything that was negative? It didn't stay that way. It made positive things happen in my life."

Determination is another key characteristic that women stated helped them to face their problems. Often cited as a resilience building block for traumatized individuals (Taylor et al. 2000; Thomas and Woodside 2011; Williams et al. 2001), determination aids in the process of moving from merely surviving to accomplishing personal growth (Williams et al. 2001). In the face of adversity, Becky is a self-described "fighter": "You're not gonna shoot me down. I'm a fighter. I hear negativity, 'You can't do this,' and I'll try to prove them wrong." When specifically asked if she saw herself as determined, she agreed, "Yeah, when I really put my mind to it, nothing can stop me and no one can stop me. I'm going to do it. Whether it be good or bad [*laughs*]." When sixty-one-year-old Meri was asked about the driving force that kept her going despite years of physical and sexual violence, homelessness and a host of other adversities, she cited her determination: "You try and you keep going until you get where you want to be."

Some women cited their intelligence as a determinant. According to these women, they were able to draw on their intelligence to help them negotiate difficult situations; others explained that their intellect served as a source of positive self-esteem. For example, Rosa stated that she used her intelligence to work out when a person or situation was harmful to her in order to help her not fall into some of the traps she saw other women falling into: "I don't like bullshit ... I'm a very, very intelligent person and I can see through all that. If you're going to waste my time, get out of the way, I got to go." Chrissie felt that she was able to survive, because "I'm a lot smarter than people give me credit for." Eve drew on her belief in her innate intelligence in order to bolster her self-esteem despite years of drugs, prison, and interpersonal and gang-related violence that might have otherwise broken her down. She was, she said, "a genius" who just happened to come from "a dysfunctional family." Similarly, Kodi credited herself as "brilliant," stating that she used her intelligence to channel her feelings about her situation into creative outlets, such as writing and plays. Anisha credited her strength to two sources: "I find myself very open. I find myself very intelligent."

Other personality traits women saw as both innate and as contributing to their emotional strength included independence, self-confidence, and the ability to connect to others. In relation to independence, when Gem was first asked what factors she attributes to her personal strength, she replied, "My character, my personality. I let it be known that I may be short, but I'm not to be played with." She then cited specific factors that included independence:

> I came in here by myself, when I leave I will be by myself. I might get a couple of the females' numbers and maybe keep in touch, develop a life-long relationship until it's our time to go, but I'm by myself. If you come with me, it's because you want to. If I go with you, it's because I want to.

Gem also exudes a tremendous degree of self-confidence, which she sees as innate and linked to her ability to be a leader: "I feel like I'm a leader at work and a leader here. I don't ride with anybody ... I don't have anything to prove." Like Kodi, who saw herself as highly artic-ulate ("I speak well"), and thus able to connect with others to form satisfactory relationships, Dagmar self-described as "pretty verbal." To illustrate how her ability to form bonds has benefited her, she said, "I've met some nice people and I've made some friends, so that's a plus. Maybe lifelong friends, I don't know. In adversity, that tends to be when people really hold it together." Dagmar not only drew positive self-esteem from her ability to make friends, but also from her willing-ness to help others: "I like to do good things for people because that's who I am." This was also true for Bianca:

> I'm good at making people smile. When they are down and out, I still go to them. It's just me. I like having fun ... When I go to different people, it's not being fake, it's still me, but just to bring that laughter and smile about ... that's what's helping me go further and further, and giving me strength. This is what gets me going and helps me rise above.

Flexibility – that is, the extent to which individuals can adapt to new situations and develop new modes of thinking and being – is another key factor associated with resilience (Barankin and Khanlou 2007). Sev-eral of the women spoke of themselves as highly adaptive individu-als who were able to draw on their ability to be flexible in order to manoeuvre the challenges they faced. Ava was one of these women, although she preferred to use the term "open minded." She saw her ability to adapt as not only helping her to survive in the present but also as a key to future growth. "Times are changing, people are changing," she said, "and you have to be willing to make a few changes. To grow. You know what I mean?" Ava then drew on the following analogy to illustrate her point: "It's like staying in a box and there's some things outside that box." When asked about her ability to adapt to the changes in her life, Valeeta, a domestic violence survivor, said, "My favourite saying to most of my friends is, 'I've been up and down so many times, I make a yo-yo look like it's standing still.'" Her attitude towards the challenges life had thrown at her was illustrated by the comment: "Get over it. Get over yourself. Pick your ass up by the bootstraps and you just keep walking."

Learned Self-Knowledge and Skills

Taking an inventory of past traumatic events, considering how those events have impacted oneself, and then contemplating how, if ever, the situation was resolved, can be a helpful process to undertake for those struggling with violence and other forms of traumatic experience (Maggio 2006). This learning process not only assists individuals in developing a sense of their own competency in dealing with stressful situations, it can also aid the development of strategies for dealing with future adversity (Maggio 2006).

Several participants spoke about the knowledge and skills they had learned and developed as a direct result of their experiences. For many of the women, one of the most important skills was learning how to set appropriate boundaries in intimate and other interpersonal relationships. When Lake was engaged in sex work, she had been involved in an intimate relationship with the man who was her pimp. She described her life then as "really hard," filled with abuse and repeated stints in the county jail. During Lake's last period of incarceration, she said, "I made some promises to myself ... I wasn't going to let anybody or anything take me down or make me feel less than." As a result, she began to set healthier boundaries and, today, says of IPV, "I don't put up with it now." Amina has learned that she needs to be surrounded by positive people and she now distances herself from people who would exploit or abuse others. "As I get older, I don't got time for that. Come and get this person. I don't want that negativity around me."

Several women said they had learned life lessons as a result of their past experiences, including that they had the strength to survive. Chrissie attributed her ability to be resilient to "foster care, you know, for so long, and then the domestic violence." Today, she says, "I'm a very strong woman ... I've had to take care of myself for so long, what do you expect?" Angela expressed gratitude for two of the struggles she faced post-victimization, because they had made her stronger:

I was telling somebody the other day, "I'm really grateful for my addiction and my mental illness [depression]." They said, "Why?" I said, "Because, I wouldn't be the person I am today." For me, it's been a great gift. You look back and you say, "Look at all the strength I acquired through that."

Tina also felt that she had learned something valuable about herself as a result of adversity: "All I know is that what makes me strong is going through all the stuff I went through. I learned from that." Ava had similarly learned that "life is a recovery program. If you can get up and try again, you're recovering." Lake was also among the women who said they had learned from their experiences. In Lake's case, she said, "I struggled with it at first. I wouldn't learn. I'd keep making the same mistakes. Now that I'm older, I try to look at life's lessons and try to learn from them." Others said they felt they had learned to become more determined in reaching goals. Angela said the "number one life lesson" she had learned was "don't give up!" Taking this as her motto, Angela – who had been a self-described "multiple drug relapser" – had been maintaining her sobriety, had recently secured housing, and was about to enrol in a trade school. Louise, who had struggled previously with completing tasks and achieving life goals, had recently revealed to her mother that her experiences of adversity had taught her how to see things through to completion: "I've learned throughout all of that I didn't have determination, and now I have it."

Participants also identified other skills or knowledge they felt they had acquired through experiences of violence and other forms of adversity. Bianca felt that her past had made her stronger and often "teaches me a lesson." She was also motivated from an awareness of the fact that she was not alone in her struggle to overcome years of physical abuse. Seeing other women coming from similar situations, she said, "Just to see them struggle [too], it boosts my motivation. Not only that, it boosts my confidence and self-esteem." Whereas some women saw flexibility as an innate trait they possessed, Angela felt that she had learned how to become more flexible in response to the various shifts and turns her life had taken. "I found through life that being flexible is the fore way to being teachable. If you're not flexible, you're not teachable, and if you're not teachable, you might as well die." Holly similarly felt that she had learned to adapt: "I've been in the hood. I've hung with the thugs, the guns, the drugs, the prostitutes, the hypes, all this. But I was able to make a beautiful woman out of that. I'm a chameleon. You might think it's a mess, but it's adapting." Like several of the women,

Brittney was in the process of learning to take interpersonal and other risks and was building self-confidence as a result. "I am not going to let fear take over my mind," she said. Instead, she was all about "trying something different ... learning to take risks," by both asking for help and trusting others. When Kodi first arrived at the shelter, she said, "I didn't think anyone cared to know me. For what?" Through time and effort, like Brittney, she learned to take risks by speaking with others, which in turn allowed her to build up her self-confidence. When asked if she now makes friends easily, she replied, "I have very, very strong interpersonal skills ... I love to hear, I love to speak, I love to talk."

Spirituality

Spirituality is frequently cited as an important factor in the development of resilience among some individuals (Williams and Lindsey 2005; Bogar and Hulse-Killacky 2006). Not only can spirituality provide an effective, pro-social outlet for dealing with one's emotions (Joseph 2011), but participation in organized religious groups can produce strong community ties and an able social support network for those struggling with violence (Joseph 2011). In addition, spirituality provides many with a sense of purpose in life (Joseph 2011). Studies of resilience among homeless and runaway youth confirm these claims. Williams and Lindsey (2005), for example, found that for some homeless youth, a sense of meaning and purpose in life as evidenced by an ability to see the "bigger picture" – manifested in faith-based or non-faith-based spirituality – was particularly helpful to achieving resilience.

Among the homeless women we interviewed, several stated they drew strength from their spiritual faith. When Caprice was asked what she sees as the source of her personal strength in facing violence and other forms of adversity, she replied, "You look to your faith." Since Gillian's experience of being abducted, she has given up drugs and turned to religious faith. When asked if she sees herself as a "strong individual," she initially replied, "No, I know I'm weak," before explaining, "when I'm weak, I'm strong [because] then it's Jesus' strength [that] takes over." Jenny had also recently "found my way back to Jesus." As a result of returning to the faith of her youth, she finds that spirituality has "been helping me a lot. That's what's keeping me going." Sandra described herself as having "self-esteem issues when I was with my ex-boyfriend ... the one who beat me." When she entered a mission-based shelter program, she began attending church and today says of herself, "Since I've been here, I feel good about myself. My self-esteem is … I know I can do all things with Christ." Similarly, Louise had recently experienced a religious conversion following a painful talk with her daughter, a talk she described as "the worst beating I've ever gotten." Finding spiritual faith has "really changed me in a way that I have been searching for," and she is now filled with a sense of peace and contentment: "My journey down that path of pain and sorrow is gone [*crying*]. I have a brighter tomorrow that is promise, peace, joy, happiness, and unconditional love." She also believes her faith provides her with the strength and resolve necessary to accomplish her goal of bettering her life: "I'm not going to give up. I'm not going to fail."

Some participants specifically cited prayer as providing a source of comfort, security, and strength. "I pray a lot," Ruby said. "It keeps me strong." Then, referring to the violence and chaos of the streets outside, she invoked the metaphor of a protective shield: "I just wear the armour of the Lord on me, when I'm out there." Nidra also uses prayer to provide her with a sense of security while she's out on the streets: "I pray and ask God to guide me and protect me and don't let no harm or danger come to me." Referring to God, Nidra added that when she feels she needs strength to help her deal with a situation, "He's the best person I can call on." Helen draws on what she sees as the power of prayer to help her deal with memories of past abuse: "I ask God to remove those things that I have no control over. Put it in my past, because that's where it is." She added, that those memories "used to eat me up, really, really bad," but through prayer and counselling, "now it's not as bad." Similarly, Brittney, who has been subjected to decades of physical abuse in various interpersonal relationships, noted that prayer brought her a sense of comfort: "Ever since I have been talking to God I have been so much better." Mariah, who struggles with anger issues following years of abuse, neglect, and sexual exploitation, noted that she relies on her spiritual faith to help her deal with daily issues and uses prayer as a tool to help her deal with memories from the past. What she does, she said, is "suck it in. Take a nice deep breath and pray that God make it okay." Like Virginia and Ava, Mariah uses her faith to engender feelings of gratitude, despite the fact that she is a nineteen-year-old homeless woman, pregnant with her first child, and carrying heavy emotional and mental burdens from abuse. "You have to think," she said, "if He [God] didn't want you here today, you didn't have to wake up. You gotta be grateful."

Family and Friends

It has been suggested that "interpersonal connectedness and support may be the single most powerful predictor of human resilience"
(Everly, McCormack, and Strouse 2012, 90). Through intimacy, shared
expressions of understanding, empathy, and other forms of social support, those struggling with the after-effects of violence can often find
additional strength and courage in initiating or remaining in the resilience process (Joseph 2011).

Friends and family members were frequently cited as the individuals
from whom women could draw strength, support, and encouragement.
Among mothers, children were seen as a strong motivating factor. Lake
noted that she uses her "kids as a leverage," meaning that she was motivated to get help for her struggles with violence and a resulting addiction because she didn't "want them to grow up and be like, 'Mommy is
a crackhead.'" Exposure to children of addicted parents in support settings had left her with the resolve that "if my son was sitting in this seat
talking about his growing up, I don't ever want my son to say, 'Well, my
mommy was smoked out.'" When Denise was asked where she draws
her strength from, she replied, "I got my son." Speaking of her son,
Bianca revealed, "He helps bring strength to me every day. He tells me
I can do things and that he loves me. He's four years old and I know I
gotta do it for him. I have to push myself for him." As may be recalled
from chapter 1, the only thing that stopped Tonya, who was in despair
following the death of her ex-husband, from taking her own life, was
the knowledge that her children would be without a mother: "My son
was like, 'Momma, I need you.' And that's what pushed me that night.
It stopped me. Otherwise, I don't think I would've been here." Renisa
had similarly had thoughts of suicide, but awareness of the emotional
and mental costs on her children stopped her: "I didn't want my kids
growing up saying, 'My momma didn't love me enough; she killed herself.' That's what kept me here."

Other women cited parents or siblings, or both, as sources of support
from whom they drew personal strength. For example, although Ruby
acknowledged that in relation to her experiences of IPV and its consequences, "I dealt with it myself," she also credited her father for making her "a strong person." Of her father she also said, "I really believed
that all the things that he was telling me, that he was teaching me, to be
strong." Having survived the violence and having broken away from
her abusive partner, Ruby concluded, "I became even stronger than I

5.1. Family, Chicago. Photo: L. Huey, 2011.

ever thought I could be." Ann described her family as people she turns to when she needs support, because "they're always uplifting." Lake also turns to her family, to whom she remains "very close," thanks to the power of social media: "We talk to each other on Facebook." Other women stay connected through regular phone calls. Louise, who is emotionally close to both her mother and her children, maintains regular contact despite being physically apart: "We talk on the phone almost every day."

Many of those living within street-based communities become part of networks of social support (Cohen 2001). Integration within such networks not only provides security but also interpersonal support and the sharing of survival skills; it also helps to reduce symptoms of loneliness and vulnerability (Molina-Jackson 2007; Whitbeck 2009). As one might expect, then, friendships were important to several of the women for fostering intimacy and social bonds, as well as for receiving emotional support. Renisa described herself as having a "friend that's my support system. He gets me through like everything," before adding,

"I have two other ones … they make me so strong today." Barb said that when she feels the weight of her problems pressing down on her, she talks to "different ministers and friends." For years, Chantelle had been carrying secrets, the burden of which led to multiple episodes of depression. First, she had been sexually assaulted as a teenager, while working for the man's family. Shortly afterwards, she began a relationship with someone else that led to a pregnancy. When Chantelle was no longer able to hide the pregnancy, her family forced her to give the baby up for adoption. What she was unable to tell her father, or anyone else, was that she had been molested and that the boy she had loved, and by whom she had become pregnant, was not of the same race. "All those years, I couldn't tell," she explained. Her silence gave way when she was befriended by Sindy at the shelter at which both were staying: "I told her [and] it lifted a weight for me to talk to her." Of the shame she had carried, she added, "it lifted." Dagmar said of some of the women at her shelter: "We support each other, those of who have become friends. When someone has a bad day, you're there for them. When someone has a meltdown, you have to give them some support."

Some of the women interviewed were presently involved in intimate relationships and view their partners as being a source of strength. Nineteen-year-old Nidra met her boyfriend, whom she described as "a nice guy," at the shelter they were both staying at. When asked about sources of emotional support she draws upon in her struggle to overcome years of childhood physical and sexual abuse, she immediately mentioned her boyfriend, providing the following example of how he tries to help her through the depressed feelings she often experiences:

> I was crying yesterday because I was depressed and he would hug me and kiss me on the cheek and say, "It's gonna be okay." He bought me this [referring to a small, stuffed animal]. Took me out to eat and to the movies. It was very, very sweet. He keeps my mind off a lot of negative things. He keeps me on the right track as far as working up to positive things.

Chrissie, who battles significant depression, also draws emotional support from her boyfriend, whom she credits with having "saved my life" during times when she had "literally wanted to walk out in front of a car." When Stephanie has things she needs to get off her chest, she turns to her boyfriend, because, she says, "[he] understands me."

There were also women without family support. As important as such support can be in overcoming violence, some traumatic events fracture victims' relationships with friends and family (Joseph 2011). In Nidra's case, she could rely on her boyfriend or on "girlfriends that I trust"; however, she was unable to talk about her ongoing struggles with the effects of physical and sexual abuse with her beloved grandmother because "sometimes she doesn't want to be hearing that type of stuff. It depresses her." Nidra was cognizant of the fact that talking about the past would "put them thoughts back into her [grandmother's] head," and she was mindful of the fact that the older woman was coping with the facts of Nidra's abuse by suppressing her thoughts and feelings about it: "She's also trying to keep it down as well about what happened to me."

We also learned that others lacked family support because family members had died or there was a substantial history of family dysfunction. Peri said she was unable to receive emotional or other support from her family, because of ongoing tensions with family members: "My family's the reason I'm here right now." Chelsea's closest relative was her father; however, he had been diagnosed with dementia and placed in a facility. Thus, she was unable to draw emotional or other support from him. Although Seven has several brothers and sisters, she does not "associate with them," and certainly does not discuss her past or present situation "because they didn't go through the stuff I went through. I went through the stuff by myself and with friends from the streets." As a result, she says, "[I am] on my own" and have been "since I was fifteen."

Although friends, particularly those with similar experiences, can provide needed support, several women lacked close friends. Cynthia said of herself, "I don't have any friends"; this sentiment was echoed by Chantelle and Kodi. Some of the women stated clearly that they chose not to have friendships because, having been betrayed in interpersonal relationships before, they were unwilling to trust others. Valerie preferred to rely solely on herself, because "it's just better." Becky was not opposed to having friends, as long as they were male. She chose not to "hang out with women all that much," because "they're all backstabbing, conniving, little bitches … like me [*laughs*]."

Community, Therapeutic, and Other Support Groups

It has been suggested that "social support is most powerful in its absence, that is, when social supports are perceived to be lacking or when they are negative in nature" (Feeny and Zoellner 2014, 331).

Although many of our participants drew strength from their friends and family, others turned to community services and support groups for guidance. In the absence of close personal relationships, such groups can function as a powerful resilience determinant (Valentine and Feinauer 1993).

The most commonly cited form of community activity women were involved in was church groups or church events. Theresa attends a local church that serves many homeless citizens. Aside from feeling connected to this institution, she enjoys the community element of church attendance and the after-service dinner: "It's just sociable."

While views as to the utility of therapy were not unanimously positive (Huey, Fthenos, and Hryniewicz 2012), several women who were attending individual therapy programs felt that the sessions provided them with new and beneficial ways of thinking about and responding to their situations. These new perspectives opened up possible strategies and tools for coping and developing new skills, from which they could derive increased self-esteem. Marion, who had spent years dealing with childhood physical and sexual abuse, and later intimate partner violence – what she described as the "recurring pattern" of violence in her life – had been unable to talk about her past, even when it manifested itself in depression and anxiety. Deeply distressed, she had sought counselling services and was open to any type of therapy that would help her move past the traumas she had experienced. Although Marion said that she could only self-identify as "strong" "sometimes," she felt that she had made some progress as a result of the therapy she had received for IPV survivors. "That's why I'm here talking to you. I can [now] open up," she explained. As a result of her positive experience with counselling, Marion described herself as being willing to participate in other therapies available to her, saying she was open to "everything that they can offer me, I need the help." Dani had been struggling until she came to her current shelter, where she received what she described as "a lot of support." Referring to the various counselling programs available, she added, "We have so many support systems here for women." As a result of this support, Dani said of herself, "now I feel very strong." Referring to her experiences of child abuse and later sexual assault, Marlys credited her therapist with giving her tools she needed to "get over it and deal with it." With the help of her therapist, she had learned "how to forgive my mother, the man who raped me." She had also forgiven her violent ex-partner for years of domestic violence. "There's different things that I've had to work out," in order to move forward, she said. "I had to be able to forgive them, to forgive myself."

Group therapy sessions were seen by many as beneficial. Mariah is a resident at a shelter for young women that offers a variety of counselling groups and programs. Mariah's favourite program is called the Inner Circle, which is directed by a woman who uses positive affirmations to bolster participants' self-esteem:

> The lady, she writes love notes that inspire you. They have to be positive. Everybody gets them. Then you get, "What do you think the purpose of life is?" You get to answer it and there's no wrong or right answer. That was my question this week. Mine was to live, grow, and become a better person. That's what you do, live, grow, laugh.

When asked if she found the affirmations helpful, she replied:

> Yes. You get little groups where everybody writes a positive note, inspirational words. It's not given to you all at once. Everything's a process. We actually exchange our love notes. So, we write 'em, turn 'em back in, and then we go around in a circle and everybody picks one.

Several of the women were in recovery programs, particularly Alcoholics Anonymous (AA) and Narcotics Anonymous (NA). Although no longer actively attending NA meetings, Candy went to meetings "for a long time" following a stint in a detox program, and has not "used drugs in, like, forever." Debbie, who had moved to Chicago on her own, is now also clean and sober and has been able to use the recovery process to create her own support system: "All my family's on the West Coast. I talked to them once in a while ... just getting clean, coming into treatment, recovery, on my own, I felt that loneliness. I was able to overcome that and create a support system on my own to where I got brothers and sisters in the program." Whenever Carmela struggles with sobriety, she reminds herself to "stay around the winners, go to 'the program,' ask for help, talk to somebody."

Conclusions

For some women, personal qualities served as key resilience determinants. Specifically, a positive attitude, determination, and intelligence were considered important in overcoming violent victimization.

Optimism, determination, and, to a lesser extent, intelligence have been identified elsewhere as key resilience determinants for those who have experienced traumatic events (Bonanno and Keltner 1997; Everly, McCormack, and Strouse 2012; Jaffee et al. 2007; Joseph 2011; Keltner and Bonanno 1997; Taylor et al. 2000; Thomas and Woodside 2011; Valentine and Feinauer 1993; Williams et al. 2001). Many women also identified their ability to learn from their experiences as essential to overcoming violence (see also Maggio 2006). For example, some women learned to avoid the people or places that led to their victimization; others, importantly, learned that they had the strength within themselves not only to survive but also to begin the process of moving forward.

For many, connections were also deemed critical resilience determinants. For example, a connection to one's spiritual self was viewed by a number of the women as an important part of their daily lives, and many credited their spiritualty as a factor in helping them achieve recovery from violence and other traumas. Faith, prayer, and the community aspects of religious practice were cited as essential to fostering personal strength and resilience. Social networks were also important resilience determinants (Bogar and Hulse-Killacky 2006; Everly, McCormack, and Strouse 2012; Joseph 2011). Although many who experience trauma and violence may lack family supports (Christiansen, Bak, and Elklit 2012; Joseph 2011), friends and family were often cited as sources that women could draw upon for strength, support, and encouragement. Women who were mothers especially discussed their children as factors motivating their desire to better themselves. In other instances, women without family support found refuge in community and support groups, including therapeutic groups and recovery programs. Sometimes, though, a lack of access to services undermined women's social support networks.

To reiterate, these determinants do not constitute a checklist for resilience. Possessing one, some, or all of the previously discussed determinants does not ensure one will recover from violence. Nevertheless, for the homeless women we spoke to, they felt it was these characteristics that made them strong women with the potential to overcome their traumatic life histories and build a better future. In the next chapter, we will look more closely at the coping strategies used by the women as they travel the path towards a promising future.

Chapter Six

Coping Strategies

I write. That's my way of meditating, is writing.

– Becky

Becky is a thirty-three-year-old Native Alaskan woman who has been homeless for most of the past four years. She is currently residing in a shelter in Los Angeles, having made the move from living on the streets, because, as she described it, "I was tired of sleeping on a tent on the sidewalk. I was really ready for a change." For many readers moving from a sidewalk to a homeless shelter might not represent much of a change; however, for Becky it meant that she was now more easily able to access housing, counselling, employment, and other services that might help her transition out of homelessness. Thus, this was, indeed, a positive step.

Becky grew up in what she described as a "really dysfunctional" family, characterized by "alcoholics, depression, drugs." Her father worked a lot and, when he was present, her home life was full of "yelling and drinking and screaming and being very abusive." As a small child, an uncle molested her; as a teenager, she was sexually assaulted. As is often the case with women who have been abused as children, the physical violence of childhood followed her into adulthood. By her own account, she has experienced "a lot of domestic violence." A few months prior to our interview, she was again sexually assaulted while living on the streets.

Becky openly admits that she has struggled with the self-esteem issues that led to drug and alcohol abuse and, in turn, to sex work. Feeling that she was overweight and unattractive as a teenager, she turned to drugs when she was eighteen. Becky explained, "I really quit smoking crack and then started smoking crystal. Then I quit doing that and gained more weight than I lost." While residing in a Los Angeles shelter, she has been engaged in several activities that have helped improve her self-esteem. For example, she is learning how to practise acceptance and to change her self-talk accordingly:

> I guess I've come to like my own skin. Before I didn't like myself, me being overweight. I've come to realize I'm a big-boned person and I've never been skinny. I'm just gonna accept the fact that I'm never gonna be skinny. Crackhead, anorexic, whatever. I'm just gonna be me. God made me that way and I'm beautiful.

Although Becky has clearly learned a lot from therapy, she credits other activities she is engaged in (including creative and other pursuits) with providing the most meaningful emotional and psychological benefits, as well as other perks. For example, Becky "recycles" – a practice otherwise known as "tinning" – which entails collecting cans and bottles and returning them to recycling depots for cash. The most important benefits of recycling, she says, are that "it puts money in my pocket and it's good exercise." To illustrate the latter, she added, "You're walking. Bending down. Lifting." Further, she explained that recycling "teaches you communication skills because you have to deal with businesses. 'What do you do with your plastic and cans? Can I please have them?'" Becky has also recently begun to explore her creative side through writing. "I figured out I'm a writer," she said. "I never used to like to write, but now I just write and it comes out as poems." Becky is able to use her poetry as a conduit for safely expressing her feelings with the result that she creates what she described as "deep, real-life poems." She also explores other facets of her creative side through visual arts: "I like to colour. I like to draw." Having learned from her mother, Becky also handcrafts Native arts: "I like to sew baby booties out of leather or seal skin." Becky's hobbies are not simply outlets that allow her to cope with the residue of the past, or the challenges of her present; they also represent to her a possible future. When asked about what she would like to be doing in the future, she had a ready answer: she wants to be "self-employed" in her own business "selling Native art."

Coping has been defined as "the behaviours and thoughts through which people attempt to manage stressful situations" (Joseph 2011, 117). Generally speaking, researchers and therapists have placed these strategies into one of two categories. The first is *approach-oriented coping* (or "engagement coping"), in which victims of violence focus their energy on improving their situation ("task-focused coping" or "problem-focused coping") and managing their emotions ("emotion-focused coping"). The second is *avoidance-oriented coping* (or "disengagement coping"), in which victims try to ignore negative feelings or situations (Joseph 2011). Of the two, researchers and clinicians have tended to view approach-oriented coping as healthy and productive and avoidance coping as maladaptive and harmful (Clements and Sawhney 2000; Calvete, Corral, and Estevez 2008).

Although our focus in this chapter is largely on approach-oriented coping – because that's what women tended to speak of when discussing their strategies for coping with violence and the stressors in their lives – this distinction between healthy and unhealthy approaches is more complicated than some might suggest. In relation to the general population, Joseph (2011) has argued that avoidance, in moderation, can be helpful by protecting survivors until they are ready to confront their trauma. With respect to homeless citizens, avoidant-coping strategies – such as consciously repressing memories or choosing not to discuss victimization – may be appropriate survival strategies given their situation, the goals they have, and the extent to which opening emotional and mental wounds might hamper achievement of those goals. Rather than treating all use of avoidant coping as signs of some type of pathology, or as manifestations of an unwillingness to begin the process of overcoming trauma or dealing with one's situation, we argue for a more nuanced approach that recognizes and responds to where individuals are "at" in the resilience process. An approach that judges coping strategies based on an individual's life circumstances, and in relation to how that person sees the effects of these strategies in terms of their own recovery, is more appropriate when considering complex populations. In other words, in keeping with the hidden resilience literature, we do not assume prima facie that what might be viewed as problematic behaviour in one context – such as refusing to seek therapy – is necessarily indicative of malfunctioning in another (Ungar 2006).

Mental Strategies

In discussing how they cope with the residual effects of the violence they had experienced, as well as with the adverse situations within which they presently found themselves, a number of the women discussed the mental strategies they employed to help them move through their lives. As was mentioned in the previous section, some individuals grappling with violence and its effects choose to actively repress their memories. Jamie was one of those who practises repression, because, she says, "right now I have to do what I need to do ... I cannot think about any negatives." Therefore, she actively chooses not to think about multiple episodes of violent victimization and other traumatic events and instead says to herself, "I'm not going to go there again [i.e., relive the past]. Let me just concentrate on this.' As much as I know it's still stuck in the back of my mind, and it ain't gonna go away, I still try not to think about it. I have lots of things to think about." Jamie says that on only one day of the year – the anniversary of her grandfather's death – is when "I do all my crying." Zoe similarly reminds herself to keep the past in the past. Referring to years of memories of physical and sexual assaults, she advised that her strategy is to say to herself, "I can't dwell on this. I've thought about it, cried about, done it and it's gone. Put it away and go on."

Sometimes women were not consciously aware they had been repressing memories or to what extent this had been occurring. Toya had been sexually assaulted by a member of her husband's family and felt unable to tell anyone what had happened for fear that she would be blamed.[1] Deciding there was little she could do about it, she chose to suppress her memories of the experience and try to move on. So successful was Toya at repressing those memories, that, when first asked if she had ever been sexually assaulted, she replied, "Nope, and I thank God for that too because I know a lot of women. Family members and all." Later in the interview, she paused and said, "You know what? I'm sorry. Yes, I was raped. And this is the crazy part ... I'm sorry ... I don't know it don't bother me like that, because I like put it in the back of my head." Truly was another example of a woman who had deeply repressed memories of her past within her mind. When asked if she had overcome the sexual abuse she had experienced as a child, she replied, "I wouldn't say I'm over it, but I don't think about it. I just don't think about it at all."

---

1 As we reported in chapter 3, the victim-blaming that worried Toya was experienced by other women. For example, Meda's husband holds her accountable for being raped. This finding is not unique to our sample – Christiansen, Bak, and Elklit (2012) found that more than one-quarter of rape victims' families perceive them to be at least somewhat responsible for being sexually assaulted.

Women like Sondra were different. They were not interested in repressing painful memories, but instead chose to use their pain and anger to drive personal and sometimes social change (see also Maggio 2006). For example, Sondra stated that not only did she feel guilt over her inability to cope with depression and addiction following years of sexual and physical violence, but that she intended to "take my guilt and do whatever I got to do because it needs to be handled. Regardless." When asked if she was using it to "fuel a rage to get out" of her situation, she responded, "I use all my pain and all my anger to keep pushing. It's all I can do." Although Erica believed that one should not dwell on the past, seeing it as counterproductive to change, she too believed that it is possible to channel the past into an energy to manifest positive changes: "You gotta do more than talk about [your past] to solve the problem. Rethink and redirect it in a different kind of way." Erica was also firmly of the view that "until you do something to make a difference, it stays the crazy same. The vicious cycle goes on."

Another frequently cited mental strategy was compartmentalization, whereby women simply set certain problems aside that they felt they were presently unable to deal with in order to address those they felt they could reasonably solve (Cordova 2008). Processing concerns in this manner can provide "opportunities to break worries down into solvable problems, face uncertainty, and make important decisions" (Cordova 2008, 195). In Dagmar's case, compartmentalization allows her to focus on managing her present to achieve her future. As she explained, "[I have] a one day at a time kind of philosophy, because you really can't look too far ahead ... you have to be focused." Erica was also a proponent of using compartmentalization to help her move forward, as she explained: "Yeah. I've been robbed. Raped. I've been in an abusive marriage ... you know what? You can't change the past. The only thing you can do is load yourself down and stress yourself out. It changes nothing."

Positive self-talk is another commonly employed strategy in managing both traumatic effects and chronic stressors (Wakai et al. 2014). Renisa, who struggles with depression, said she uses self-talk to convince herself that things are more positive than she might otherwise perceive them to be. Using the analogy of a glass being half empty or half full, she explained, "I try to say it's half full when really I'm feeling like it's half empty. I try to make myself think positive." When Valeeta feels sad or bad for herself and her present situation, she tells herself, "Regardless of how bad you think you got it, get off that pity potty. There's someone out there a lot worse off than you are." As evidenced by the following quote, Holly also uses self-talk to reorient her thinking: "You can't stunt my growth because I don't have time. My kids don't have time. The world doesn't have time." Leslie uses self-talk as a tool to help her overcome her feelings of inadequacy, which can lead to negative interactions with others. "This is basically what I tell myself: 'It's okay. I'm going to learn. Just be gentle. Be nice.'" Rather than lashing out at others, she tells herself, "Do my best not to leave a gnarly wake of destruction. It's okay if I don't know [something], just as long as I don't leave you and our interaction in a negative." Peri uses memories of her past, combined with self-talk, as a motivational tool: "I sometimes find myself coming back to where I started, to help me and boost me up to say, 'You don't want to end up back here again.'"

Letting It Out

Not all of the women used avoidance and compartmentalization techniques. Indeed, some, like Leslie, took a conventional approach and felt that mentally separating themselves from their past experiences was unhealthy. Referring to her own painful past, Leslie said, "Keeping it in just makes you sick." As a result, she says she uses "tangible actions to help myself," including discussing that past with others. "I've let it out."

Other women, like Joy, saw the interview itself as an opportunity to open up about past traumas and to begin the process of healing through "letting it out." Joy had struggled with suicidal thoughts following a sexual assault and failed marriage and was hoping to access counselling services soon. "I know I need to talk about it," she said. "That's why I'm talking to you." Samantha similarly revealed that she had struggled with depression and suicidal thoughts but had been unwilling to share this fact with doctors or counsellors. When asked why she had been willing to confide these things to an interviewer, she replied, "Maybe I needed to tell someone. That's a form of cleansing, I guess." Naomi was willing to open up during an interview in order to possibly learn something with which she could help improve herself and her situation. When asked why she had not told counsellors about her history of sexual assault and gang-related violence, she explained:

NAOMI: It be that I don't want to talk about it because of the various times I've been denied in myself. It doesn't allow me to protect myself from it.

INTERVIEWER: Because if you open up and trust somebody they could hurt you, right?

NAOMI: Right. I build a wall around myself so that I don't open up to too many people and they try to possess me.

INTERVIEWER: Why did you trust me enough to tell me?

NAOMI: Because I'm always open to change. I'm always open to help for others, as well as myself. I'm always looking for hope for others and myself. That's the reason I sat to talk with you.

While some might view Naomi's avoidance of therapy as self-defeating, previous research with homeless women reveals that many rightly fear two things: first, that opening emotional wounds might lead to an emotional or mental decline that could jeopardize present or future goals, and second, that the act of sharing with a shelter counsellor or other staff member could lead to undesirable gossip, and potential vulnerability, in relations with other residents (Huey et al. 2014; Huey 2016). In that light, Naomi's willingness to share with the interviewer, who would leave and not return, is a rational situational response.

For those who are unwilling to share with others, journalling has been shown to be a therapeutic mode of "letting out" one's thoughts and feelings. For example, in one experiment, participants were randomly assigned to write about a traumatic experience or a trivial matter (Francis and Pennebaker 1992). Although those who wrote about their traumatic experiences reported some distress at the time of writing, by the six-week follow-up all distress had dissipated, and at a six-month follow-up participants described the experience as positive and one that allowed them to gain new insights into their lives (Francis and Pennebaker 1992). Other researchers have reached similar conclusions, finding that journalling produces social, emotional, and physical health benefits for those coping with stressful life events (Lepore and Greenberg 2002). Among the women interviewed, we noted that several were actively engaged in journalling. For example, fifty-eight-year-old Salma battles with depression following years of IPV. For Salma, "journalling is good." Although she has since stopped, while Chrissie was out on the streets, she kept a journal. "If I actually write things down, getting it out on paper can actually be a big help," she shared. Sunny uses her phone as a diary in which she only journals positive things that have happened to her, so that she can go back later and read them and remind herself of "something special about that day that really got me through." As these women alluded to, it is believed that talking or writing about traumatic experiences accomplishes two goals. First, confronting the topic directly reduces active inhibition, which reduces stress associated with the inhibition. Second, putting a traumatic experience into words can set into motion a number of cognitive changes that promote health and well-being (Francis and Pennebaker 1992).

Keeping Busy

Another commonly employed coping strategy is what the women called "keeping busy," or what Klitzing (2004, 493) has termed "diversionary activities." Nadia's reasoning for coping in this way was simple: "You have to keep busy or lose your mind." Ava offered the following explanation of why "keeping busy" is important to her: "I don't like a whole lot of idle time; it makes you think about the things that are wrong." Talitha similarly said, "I just try to keep myself busy, like working or going to school" in order to avoid thinking about the years of violence and other adversities she had experienced. Talitha added, "As long as I keep myself busy I don't really think about it. I get angry and frustrated at times, but it's not worth it. I still got my whole life ahead of me." Conversely, she felt that "dwelling on the past is not really doing anything for my future." For Talitha, going to school or working, or doing both, focused her thoughts and was helping her to achieve personal goals, including moving out of homelessness and beyond a past filled with violence.

As with other coping strategies termed forms of "avoidance," researchers disagree about the benefits of keeping busy. As we have previously noted, consciously avoiding one's problems is sometimes considered unhealthy (Herman 1992; Joseph 2011). Nevertheless, others have observed that "keeping busy" – through school, work, the pursuit of leisure activities, or community volunteering – can minimize stress in the immediate aftermath of violent victimization as well as stress associated with homelessness (Frazier and Burnett 1994; Klitzing 2004). We would further add that keeping busy by occupying oneself with productive pro-social tasks – such as those undertaken by Talitha – can produce positive emotional, mental, and financial benefits.

We note that women engaged in a diverse range of activities to keep themselves busy. Ann enjoys reading: "I get into a good novel, because I need a balance. I love a good, gory novel. But I balance myself with my studies, my Bible, my journal." Holly returned to school to finish her high school diploma before taking business management classes. Bennie stays busy with a wide range of activities: "Jogging and reading ... I've supported a church group, volunteered, bake sales."

Several of the women participated in volunteer work, from which they received both a mental break from their problems and the opportunity to feel good about helping others. Patterson and Tweed (2009, 846) reported high ratings for the "realization of their own abilities and potential to offer something to the world" as an important factor in escaping homelessness. Ava, who stays at one of the shelters in Los Angeles's Skid Row district, volunteers at the local women's centre. In Chicago, Ruby was involved in volunteer work with special needs adults, of which she said, "The work is so rewarding and makes me even more humble." Ruby was also involved in an afterschool mentoring program for teenaged girls: "I taught sewing ... me and another lady taught fifteen girls." Participation in this program provided Ruby with an escape from time that might otherwise be spent in boredom, isolation, reliving the past or worrying over the future, and it also allowed her to have what she saw as a "normal" identity while she was teaching, rather than being a homeless, and therefore stigmatized, other. Dagmar also saw her volunteer work as a way to connect with others and to reconnect with her former identity as a teacher and therefore as a "normal" person:

> I like to remember who I am, even with the craziness around me. So, I volunteer. I used to teach GED, so I'm helping with the GED program here. So, I volunteer to help tutor people that are trying to get their GED. That's about me and focusing on what I need to do. It helps me to remember who I am. What my real life is supposed to look like. This is not our real life. This is where we are right now ... Even here you still have skills, things you can offer other people. If you don't lose that, you still have a powerful connection to who you are.

Aside from volunteering at church activities, Bennie described herself as a "sister keeper" – that is, as someone who enjoys "doing what I can to make life a little easier for my sisters around me." To that end, three times a week she volunteers to help organize the women's showers at her shelter: "It keeps me positive and not forget that God is preparing me for something greater. It is a challenge, but we have to remember that spirit and not get side tracked."

For several of the women, "keeping busy" also meant engaging in various physical activities for health, relaxation, social, and other benefits. Physical activity and exercise have both been shown to be positive methods of keeping busy following traumatic experiences. Indeed, "exercise is healthy in itself, but it can also provide a distraction and free up your mind when it most needs a break" (Joseph 2011, 179). Angela, who is active in her church, has a standing date with "some of the women at my church, some of my friends" to walk around the Rose Bowl twice a week. Tina loves working out and sees exercise as providing both physical and mental benefits. When asked what activities she likes to engage in, she responded, "Everything. Machines. Yoga. Jogging not too much anymore, but just pretty much the whole gambit. Weight lifting." Whitney described herself as "a very physical person," who was living in a shelter in which "about all I can do here is exercise," so she takes advantage of the opportunity to blow off steam and spend time with friends. Sharleen is also interested in physical fitness and does sit ups every night. She also does "a lot of [other] things to stay active," when she's able, including swimming.

Creative Activities

Creative activities serve multiple purposes in the lives of homeless women. In many instances, they represent forms of self-expression through which women can safely explore their thoughts and feelings (Thomas et al. 2011). They can also provide a means of relaxation within spaces that can often be loud, chaotic, or volatile. The products of their creativity provide some with opportunities to enhance their self-esteem, to make money, or to fashion for themselves a positive identity as an artist.

Dale is an example of a woman who self-identifies as "an artist." Homeless now for twelve years, she had previously worked as a nurse, but had to quit working after complications due to surgery. It was while recuperating that Dale first took up making art: "They would bring me pencils and stuff like that, a computer and paint. And from there it just didn't stop." Today, she works in several different media: "I produce art on canvas. Sculpting. Crafting. Jewellery." Kodi is an actor and writer, who produces poetry and is penning a one-woman play based on her life. One of her creations, of which she is particularly proud, is a poem entitled "Skid Row Sister" that "tells you about that kind of life." Of having this form of outlet, Kodi said, "It's so good to have this." Kodi has also recently discovered a love of creating graphic art.

"Graphic art, is my thing," she enthused. "This is the one thing I found in this lifetime that I'd been passionate about." For Mariah, pottery-making is a cathartic experience: "I love pottery now. You can just push the peddle down and let all your anger go out. You can have a lot of anger in you and build something so beautiful." Mariah similarly uses music as vehicle to let her emotions out: "I might turn on my music and just scream."

Other women spoke of the relaxation they find in engaging in various creative outlets. For example, Meri likes to write in her journal to relax. Katherine relaxes by designing clothes and through writing and singing. Ruby sews for herself and for other people, seeing craftwork as "good therapy" and as an outlet she "can throw myself into ... and distract myself." When Beth was asked if there's an activity she likes to do to make herself feel better, she replied, "I doodle."

Quiet Spaces

Life on the streets and in shelters is typically full of people, noise, and chaos, which generates significant stress for many homeless citizens (Klitzing 2004). Not surprisingly, women often felt the need to seek out quiet spaces or moments in which they could relax, collect their thoughts, pray, or simply be alone.

Nadia likes to go to the beach or to other parts of Los Angeles and "just sit there," soaking up what she sees as "a better vibe" than what she experiences at her shelter. Beth, who has a car, said that even "though gas is slightly pricey," she finds it helpful to "drive a little extra" and think about her problems in the car. Charlie has a specific destination and activity that bring her peace: fishing at the beach. For Charlie, being able to "take my line and throw it in the water and sit there ... is a good sedative. The waves from the ocean ... watching those waves is very soothing." Several of the women had accessed community yoga classes and, like Dagmar, found these classes useful for providing necessary relaxation: "It's interesting we just had a yoga class yesterday that I found really helpful ... I do meditation. I find it very relaxing, very centring. Focus internally on what's going on for you."

For the more introverted women, having a sense of peaceful solitude was deemed to be particularly necessary for their mental and emotional well-being. In her bestselling book, *Quiet: The Power of Introverts in a World That Can't Stop Talking*, Susan Cain (2013) explains the need of introverts to experience moments of solitude. For example, she describes the pitfalls of modern open-concept offices for introverts who need a quiet space to reflect and recharge, and the importance of having a quiet space to refresh and rejuvenate after a period of socializing. In comparison to most people, it is much harder for homeless introverts to find such spaces, but their importance is not diminished. Emily said that she needed the serenity that comes from having quiet moments because such times help replenish her energies, leaving her feeling, "like I'm strong, like I can cope with anything." Dana is a self-described "loner," who finds communal life difficult some times. To escape, she takes trips on the bus to various destinations: "A lot of times people think you're going on the bus because you're trying to waste time, because that's all we have is time. I would do it because I wanted to be alone. I wanted to be left alone for a while. You wanted to be somewhere by yourself." What Dana receives from her bus trips is "peace of mind." Clarita likes to meditate but also finds it difficult to find sufficient peace and quiet in shelters. Instead, she goes to the women's centre to do yoga or she just starts "walking, walking, walking." Leslie also goes to the women's centre to practise yoga: "Yoga is fabulous because you have to learn to be still and focus. It's good for you." When yoga isn't available, she says, she and her husband also "do a lot of walking. A lot of that's exhausting. We take walks. Lots of walks."

Symbolism

Referring to classic work by Fidler and Fidler (1963) on "object relations," Creek and Lougher (2008) observed that material objects can have both actual and symbolic meanings for individuals. Using the example of a shawl worn by a woman on a city bus, they noted that the shawl may not only keep her warm but also it could serve as a symbolic barrier or protective device within which she could cocoon and keep the world at bay.

Several of the women spoke of material possessions that held special meaning for them, and from which they were able to draw strength or comfort, or that provided them with a sense of hope during difficult times. Often, these symbols were artefacts from their pre-homeless lives that they managed to keep. Angela has several of these items from her time in Texas:

> I went there on faith. I had no money. God put it in my heart to make these stones with different stuff on 'em. "Obey." "Love." All kinds of different

6.1. Teddy bear, Chicago. Photo: L. Huey, 2011.

stuff. I had this one stone and it says "Peace." I went and picked up stones from the quarry. I painted 'em with nail polish and wrote on 'em with markers ... It just calms me down. I also have a picture somebody painted me. Also, when I was in Texas, I saw this young girl and I said, "Make me a picture. Just for me." She drew a picture of a flower. All different colour petals and this one blue petal and underneath the blue it said "Purpose." She said, "That's you. This is the world around you and you'll always have a purpose." So, that's on my wall.

Nadia carries with her a stuffed miniature unicorn that she has "had since I was born." Conversely, Mindy's teddy bear is of more recent origin: "I got it last Christmas at Venice Beach." She explained, "I just latched on and it just was something ... I needed it ... I just grabbed it and held it the whole day and I just wouldn't let go." The bear provides Mindy with a sense of security in spaces that she might otherwise feel unsafe in, "I keep it and I sleep with it."

Often, the symbolic items the women carried or kept in their personal spaces were related to children from whom they were separated. When Stephanie was asked about lucky scarves or other personal mementos she used to help her get through tough times, she responded, "I have these pictures of my kids ... I've got two – two actual paper pictures of my girls now that I carry with me." The symbolism of being able to carry these pictures for Stephanie was particularly poignant: "Out of everything I've lost ... 'cause I've ... I've lost everything ... I've been able to maintain and hold on to two pictures, one of each girl."

Conclusions

The women employed a variety of strategies to cope with their situations. Many of the more common strategies are what is termed "avoidance-based coping" (Joseph 2011), such as compartmentalization or focusing on short-term solvable problems rather than on one's larger problems (i.e., dealing with the effects of trauma, which can be overwhelming for women without adequate support and resources). Many women also tried to repress painful memories related to their past histories of violent victimization or other traumatic experiences, either by not thinking about the past or by focusing on other things they saw as more positive. Another popular coping strategy among our participants involved keeping busy (Klitzing 2004). Although considered maladaptive by some (Joseph 2011), keeping busy, along with repressing memories and avoiding thinking about one's problems can be seen to be a highly rational, indeed adaptive, response in light of the particular context in which the women live – that is, in frequently loud, chaotic spaces where it is not uncommon for interpersonal disputes and sometimes violence to break out (Klitzing 2004; Huey and Ricciardelli 2016).

To be clear, many of these same women, as well as other participants, also engaged in a number of coping strategies typically endorsed by the therapeutic community. For example, a number were involved in creative outlets, which are seen as an effective and safe way in which victims of violence can express themselves (Thomas et al. 2011).

What the above suggests is that the binary distinction between approach-avoidant coping and adaptive-maladaptive responses to stress and trauma may be overly simplistic for populations with a high rate of trauma and a number of cumulative stressors. In her work on trauma and recovery, Herman (1992) strongly encourages confronting one's negative experiences, treating avoidance as a maladaptive response to stress. It is possible, though, that the sheer volume of stressors faced by homeless female victims of violence necessitates repressing some of their most painful memories in order to address other problems they face. Thus, while repressing memories may be maladaptive in other populations, it can be a necessary survival tactic for other individuals and groups. Likewise, focusing on manageable problems – like finding food or a place to sleep – while ignoring a lengthy victimization history can be necessary to survival and may be demonstrative of a hidden resilience.

Chapter Seven

Building on Strengths

In this book, we have attempted to provide a more nuanced image of homeless women. Drawing upon the experiences of many women, we observed lives rife with episodes of violent victimization, but also women who possessed a clear desire to overcome the effects of those experiences and to "move on" from both violence and homelessness. Within the remaining pages of this book, we review our key findings in order to advance three specific recommendations for helping women achieve their goals based on their circumstances. We see these recommendations as critical to helping women achieve resilience, particularly those who might be otherwise struggling. The first recommendation is to increase awareness of resilience as a process – one that must take into account the unique situation of many homeless citizens in contrast to more general populations. The second is the use of strength-based programs within social work settings. The third is to support women on the pathways to becoming strong by increasing women's ability to access social services and by improving their physical and ontological security through affordable housing.

Summing Up

The participants whose stories comprise the contents of this book had varied life histories. Nevertheless, all of these women had experienced extensive victimization in their lives. For several, their familiarity with violence began in childhood, sometimes continuing into adulthood; other women escaped childhood victimization, but lived through considerable violence as adults. Often, those within the women's own families and social networks perpetrated violence against them, resulting in not only physical injury but also deep emotional scars from the betrayal of their trust and love (see also Browne and Bassuk 1997; Tischler, Rademeyer, and Vostanis 2007). Our participants' experiences of victimization included IPV, sexual assault in childhood and adulthood, non-intimate partner physical violence, and gang-related violence. Further, more than 80 per cent of our participants had experienced *multiple* forms of violence within and across childhood and adulthood, and many had also witnessed serious violence inflicted onto others.

The women interviewed openly discussed the emotional scars that lingered long after their physical injuries had healed. Symptoms commonly associated with depression and anxiety, alcohol and drug addiction, and PTSD were common, and experiencing multiple episodes of homelessness was considered a corollary of victimization. Women also described how being victimized distorted their beliefs about themselves and others. Feelings of shame, distrust, and self-doubt were common – many women blamed themselves for being physically or sexually assaulted and, sometimes, their family blamed them, too.

Despite facing significant challenges, most of our participants were engaged in the recovery process in some way. Developing resilience is, indeed, a *process,* and a nonlinear and often cyclical one at that (Joseph 2011). Similarly, the process of transitioning away from the streets has been characterized by slow overall gains in the context of significant setbacks (Kidd et al. 2016). On both fronts, women encountered both practical and emotional roadblocks. For example, women could experience stability and feel well, but then run into an old acquaintance, encounter some kind of trigger and reopen old emotional wounds. Others lost jobs and worried about their income security, causing financial hardship and increased anxiety. Some women experienced victimization (once again), and saw feelings of hopelessness re-emerge. Cycling in and out of homelessness, other women, like Renisa, felt that despite their best efforts, they just couldn't "get it together." Notwithstanding these obstacles, many of the homeless women presented in the preceding pages maintained unwavering optimism about their future – they were certain they would succeed in their journey and thus would say with confidence "things are gonna get better somehow."

As we discussed in chapter 5, factors that increase women's likelihood of experiencing a degree of resilience post-victimization are known as resilience determinants. Several innate personality characteristics were noted as determinants among our participants, including a positive outlook, determination, and intelligence or "street smarts."

Women also described "learning from their past," and talked about their choices – such as avoiding people or situations that could put them at risk – as being integral to moving forward.

Recovering from trauma can be facilitated through the development of coping skills, when women learn what works for them, and when they are able to process and learn from experience. Our participants found various ways to cope with their respective situations. For example, writing was described as cathartic by some women; others described how sharing their story with peers or professionals had been a turning point. Some women found outlets for their energy and worries through volunteering, exercising, or community involvement, while other experienced a sense of empowerment and of moving on through pursuing dreams, by returning to school or by securing employment.

Not all coping strategies used by our participants are conventionally thought of as healthy responses to trauma. Indeed, many such strategies are viewed as outright maladaptive; however, they seemed to help these women cope. For example, long-term compartmentalization – or avoiding a problem entirely – is considered a maladaptive response to stress. Likewise, repressing negative thoughts and memories is considered unhealthy (Herman 1992; Joseph 2011), but several women described pushing aside painful memories or simply not thinking about certain things. Other women tried to keep busy to avoid thinking about their problems and violent pasts. Why might these unhealthy coping strategies, in addition to some healthy strategies, work for these women? We suggest that a binary distinction between approach-avoidant coping and adaptive-maladaptive responses to stress may be too simplistic when considering populations with extraordinary cumulative stressors.

Remembering That Resilience Is a Relative Process

The majority of the 187 survivors of violence discussed in this book identified as strong women in part *because* their experiences of trauma and poverty taught them valuable lessons about life and about themselves. As many have noted before, adversity is a notoriously good teacher. The point, however, is not to glorify or romanticize the value of women suffering through horrible experiences of violence. Rather, we seek to aid in the shift taking place in relation to discussions of feminized poverty, a shift away from a past focus on pathologies and maladaptive behaviours (such as addiction, mental health, refusal to engage with trauma) and towards a new focus on the key factors that can support women's recovery. Such a shift, we believe, will help us to generate a better understanding of how to facilitate resilience within this portion of the population, which we hope will, in turn, reduce cycles of homelessness.

Some of the earliest literature on the development of resilience offered views as to the best ways in which to respond to trauma. These views were subsequently adopted by many within therapeutic, social work and other communities as cardinal rules to be followed. Among these was the belief that recovery from violence could only be achieved through remembering and expressing horrific experiences (Herman 1992). Indeed, a work frequently cited as a landmark in the trauma field quite clearly states that recovery from trauma should not be confused with "banishing [traumatic memories] from consciousness," as the latter is not helpful and will impede the recovery process (Herman 1992, 1). In research for the projects that inform this book, one of the authors was told by homeless women on multiple occasions that the fear of having to relate their experiences in detail was a primary reason they chose not to seek therapy when it was otherwise available to them (Huey, Fthenos, and Hryniewicz 2012). Their rationale was simple: they saw the act of being forced to relive painful memories as retraumatizing and a process that would likely derail whatever progress they had made towards recovering and escaping homelessness (Huey, Fthenos, and Hryniewicz 2012). Intuitively, they knew something that research studies and clinical experience have validated: for individuals with complex traumatic histories, confronting traumatic events while dealing with chronic stressors – such as homelessness and the issues that status can bring – is retraumatizing for many (Frazier and Burnett 1994; Maté 2008; Brown 2008). Thus, what may work with individuals in other segments of the population is not necessarily useful or helpful when responding to traumatized individuals trying to cope within highly adverse situations. Resilience is not just a process; rather, it is a process that is highly contingent upon who and where one finds her or himself.

In discussing "hidden resilience" (Ungar 2006) and its use within the literature, we have already made a point about the relative nature of resilience as a construct, so why reiterate this point here? We contend that strengths-based approaches should guide responses to women's needs, but it is important to remember that what constitutes a "strength" will be context-dependent (Brown 2008). This is also the case with respect to coping strategies. As research on homeless youth has demonstrated, some coping strategies that are easily dismissed as unhealthy or counter-productive within mainstream society represent viable survival strategies and signs of adaptation to street-based environments (Bender et al. 2007). It bears repeating: dichotomizing coping as healthy versus unhealthy may not be useful for populations like the homeless female survivors of violence discussed in this book. A focus on such dichotomies within therapeutic or social work environments oversimplifies these women's lives and may undermine the goal of helping them to identify personal and social strengths, build self-esteem, and move forward in a positive fashion.

Trauma Informed Care and Strengths-Based Approaches

Over the past two decades, there has been a significant shift in therapeutic and social work theory and practice, moving away from an earlier focus on individual pathology, dysfunction, disorder, and moral or other failings towards an emphasis on strengths, well-being, resources, and positive forms of mental health provision (Coulter 2014). Part of this shift has been a growing recognition of the role of trauma in creating personal distress and a commensurate movement towards the adoption of what has been termed trauma informed care (TIC). Trauma informed care has been defined as "a broad approach to human services systems in which all aspects of program culture and service delivery are designed to be responsive to the effects of trauma" (Wilson, Fauci, and Goodman 2015, 587). One significant way in which TIC marks a radical departure from other, more traditional forms of practice is that services provided under the umbrella of TIC are not intended to solely manage or treat the mental or emotional symptoms resulting from violent victimization and other traumatic events; rather, they are meant to embody a holistic approach that is "welcome and appropriate to the special needs of trauma survivors" (Harris and Fallot 2001, 5).

What does a TIC model encompass? While there is no one particular vision, there *is* relatively common agreement concerning some key features. Among these is an emphasis on trauma awareness that is embedded throughout all service domains (from individual interventions to policies and programs) (Wilson, Fauci, and Goodman 2015). Linked to such awareness must be a "recognition of how trauma can destroy a sense of safety and personal power in relationships" (Lewinson, Thomas, and White 2014, 202). This recognition should be manifest in client-centred approaches that empower women by addressing their needs for physical and psychological safety and through efforts aimed at maximizing women's sense of autonomy and choice throughout the process (Lewinson, Thomas, and White 2014; see also Hopper, Bassuk, and Olivet 2010). In summarizing the relevant literature, Mackenzie-Mohr, Coates, and McLeod (2012, 138) note that in such models, service providers treat women with dignity and respect as well as form an underlying assumption that "the impact of trauma is far-reaching" and influences both "personal development and coping strategies." Similarly, providers should also take into account women's life experiences and how those experiences may impact where they are at in the recovery process and which coping strategies they use, and also their relative social positions and environmental and cultural contexts (Mackenzie-Mohr, Coates, and McLeod 2012). These tenets of TIC are well-suited for the complex lives of the homeless women whose stories make up this book. Further, therapy itself can, and ideally should, take many forms, thus maximizing women's choices. These forms might include individual counselling, group work, arts and crafts, dance, theatre, creative writing, or any other type of program or activity that can promote healing through creating, sharing, self-expression, and self-esteem building (Iveson and Cornish 2016).

Another key component of TIC approaches, and one that is especially relevant in light of the content presented in this book, is a focus on client strengths (Coulter 2014). Strengths-based interventions and programs are intended to foster the development of a client's resilience through the identification and nurturing of individual strengths and supports that can facilitate recovery (Thompson, McManus, and Voss 2006; McManus and Thompson 2008). Following from the notion of resilience as relative and as a process, the role of the service provider is to aid in helping to build on "unrecognised or under-appreciated strengths and resources," so that a woman might consciously draw on these internal and external resources in dealing with both the after-effects of trauma and other current challenges (Coulter 2014, 51). The nurturance of strengths can also help women in forming a more positive, empowered stance to their problems, and facilitate the building of self-esteem. Although we were unable to locate an evidence base that specifically demonstrates the effectiveness of strengths-based models for homeless women, we do note that a growing body of research shows that homeless youth can benefit greatly from such approaches (Bender et al. 2007), particularly when individual strengths are identified in order to develop targeted solutions to specific problems (Bender et al. 2007; see also McManus and Thompson 2008).

It has been said that "utilizing a strengths-based approach can assist homeless youth in looking toward the future with the belief that they have the power to effect positive change in their lives and transition out of homelessness" (Bender et al. 2007, 39). Evidence from interview data presented in this book shows that homeless women not only have strengths upon which they can build – even when struggling with multiple and often highly complex challenges – but also many intuitively do so in order to try to overcome the effects of violent victimization. It should be abundantly clear that such women would benefit greatly from strengths-based therapeutic and social work wrapped in a broader trauma-informed approach. However, therapeutic services, let alone trauma-informed programs for homeless victims of violence, remain too few.

For women experiencing the emotional and psychological effects of trauma – anxiety, depression, and PTSD among them – the ability to engage in therapy, programming, and counselling *on their own terms* can be critical to a successful outcome (Padgett et al. 2008). Allowing women to set the agenda for casework, counselling, and other human service interventions is preferable to approaches that might pathologize women by focusing near-exclusively on the negative aspects of their current behaviours and functioning, such as addiction issues or mental health problems (Bebout 2001). For too long, the continuum of care approach has imposed "therapeutic projects" on women, such as achieving sobriety or agreeing to deal with mental health issues – regardless of self-assessed needs – *before* providing access to housing or other economic and social supports women actually want (Culhane and Metraux 2008; Tsemberis, Gulcur, and Nakae 2004; Goering et al. 2014). By way of contrast, TIC – which emphasizes client-led approaches, building on women's strengths, and treating women in trauma recovery as co-equal to therapists and other practitioners – can help restore women's dignity, develop their self-esteem, and more effectively meet their individual needs.

Supporting Homeless Women to Become Strong

While service providers who recognize resilience as a relative process and use strengths-based TIC approaches hold considerable process, their value for supporting homeless survivors of violence in "'moving on" is significantly undermined if women cannot access their services. To be sure, issues surrounding lack of access to therapeutic and other services available to homeless women have been detailed elsewhere (Huey and Ricciardelli 2016; Huey, Fthenos, and Hryniewicz 2012; Huey et al. 2014), but it is nevertheless important to recognize deficits within current service systems for homeless citizens. Simply put, access to support services for homeless women ought to be improved to foster their pathways to becoming "strong."

As was discussed in chapter 5, some of the women interviewed were able to access psychiatric services, counselling, or other forms of therapy, and these services were perceived as helpful in nurturing resilience among these women. However, such services were not universally available, sometimes did not have hours that were compatible with a woman's schedule, and were fraught with other practical barriers (Huey et al. 2014). Further, when services are available, there is frequently a lack of choice. Some programs are group-based only, which can represent a barrier for individuals who are fearful about speaking in group settings or who are concerned about issues of confidentiality. Others rely on therapy forms that may make some women feel uncomfortable or even disempowered (Dietz 2000; Huey, Fthenos, and Hryniewicz 2012). Even when counselling and other therapeutic services are available and accessible, intake and other service workers often neglect to include even basic questions about victimization and other forms of traumatic experience in interviews with women (Huey et al. 2014). In doing so – or, more accurately, in failing to do so – service workers devalue a prime opportunity to learn about underlying traumas that homeless women have experienced and to understand those events and circumstances that women are working towards overcoming. As a result, opportunities to reduce exposure to conditions that may undermine women's functioning or development (e.g., people, places, or circumstances that trigger painful memories), or to introduce interventions that target adaptive change and that support strength building may be squandered (Masten 2011).

The above recommendations – understanding resilience as a process, drawing upon strengths-based TIC models, and accessible and supportive social services that promote resilience – should not be read as ignoring a crucial fact: a woman's ability to engage in healing work and become strong can be significantly impeded by continued homelessness and the physical and ontological insecurity that state of existence brings, as well as by feelings of social isolation and a lack of peer support, medical, therapeutic, and other resources that serve as resilience determinants or promote coping (Padgett et al. 2008). That the women in our study pushed forward in life *despite being homeless* and, therefore, without access to stable, safe, quiet spaces in which to heal and cultivate their potential is a testament to their strength, but this does not belie the fact that impoverished women require a safe space to call "home." For many of the women in our study, violence led to homelessness which led to more violence. Personal safety in the environment of "the street" is challenging, if not impossible, for homeless women (Wardhaugh 1999; Huey and Quirouette 2010). If, as Herman (1992) tells us, physical safety is necessary for complete recovery from trauma, then we are obliged to help women who are still struggling with homelessness and becoming "strong" find secure housing. Indeed, our findings lend support to calls for more affordable and accessible housing and for support of Housing First initiatives[1] (Padgett, Gulcur, and Tsemberis 2006; Culhane and Metraux 2008; Wagner and Gilman 2012; Goering et al. 2014).

Final Thought

We wish to conclude this book by offering a single idea: hope. As the stories described in these pages amply demonstrate, hope is a significant motivator for positive change and, in many cases, is the only thing that some women have left. Programs and services that sustain hope, and that fuel wellness, promote recovery and offer stability, need to be considered. Hope is not only essential to trauma recovery, but is fundamental to the ability of these women to succeed in building a better future.

---

1 "Housing First (HF) is an evidence-based intervention model, originating in New York City (Pathways to Housing), that involves the immediate provision of permanent housing and wrap-around supports to individuals who are homeless and living with serious mental illness, rather than traditional 'treatment then housing' approaches" (Goering et al. 2014, 6).

References

American Psychological Association (APA). 2013. *Diagnostic and Statistical Manual of Mental Disorders*. 5th ed. Washington, DC: APA.

Anderson, Debra G., and Margaret M. Imle. 2001. "Families of Origin of Homeless and Never Homeless Women." *Western Journal of Nursing Research* 23 (4): 394–413. https://doi.org/10.1177/019394590102300406.

Anderson, Elijah. 1999. *Code of the Street: Decency, Violence, and the Moral Life of the Inner City*. New York: W.W. Norton.

Baker, Charlene K., Sarah L. Cook, and Fran H. Norris. 2003. "Domestic Violence and Housing Problems: A Contextual Analysis of Women's Help-Seeking, Received Informal Support, and Formal System Response." *Violence Against Women* 9 (7): 754–83. https://doi.org/10.1177/1077801203009007002.

Baker, Charlene K., Kris A. Billhardt, Joseph Warren, Chiquita Rollins, and Nancy Glass. 2010. "Domestic Violence, Housing Instability, and Homelessness: A Review of Housing Policies and Program Practices for Meeting the Needs of Survivors." *Aggression and Violent Behavior* 15 (6): 430–9. https://doi.org/10.1016/j.avb.2010.07.005.

Baker, John P., and Howard Berenbaum. 2007. "Emotional Approach and Problem-focused Coping: A Comparison of Potentially Adaptive Strategies." *Cognition and Emotion* 21 (1): 95–118. https://doi.org/10.1080/02699930600562276.

Bandura, Albert. 1971. *Social Learning Theory*. New York: General Learning Press.

Barankin, Tatyana, and Nazilla Khanlou. 2007. *Growing Up Resilient: Ways to Build Resilience in Children and Youth*. Toronto: Centre for Addiction and Mental Health.

Barker-Collo, Suzanne L. 2001. "Adult Reports of Child and Adult Attributions of Blame for Childhood Sexual Abuse: Predicting Adult

Adjustment and Suicidal Behaviors in Females." *Child Abuse & Neglect* 25 (10): 1329–41. https://doi.org/10.1016/S0145-2134(01)00278-2.

Bassuk, Ellen L., Jennifer N. Perloff, and Ree Dawson. 2001. "Multiply Homeless Families: The Insidious Impact of Violence." *Housing Policy Debate* 12 (2): 299–320. https://doi.org/10.1080/10511482.2001. 9521407.

Bassuk, Ellen. L., K. Bennett, T. Bernstein, L. Davis, A.V. Denton, M.E. Grandin, S. Hills, A. Lezak, T. Murphy, A. Steacy, and S. Zerger. 2010. *Services in Supportive Housing 2010 Annual Report*. Rockville, MD: Homeless Programs Branch, Division of Service and Systems Improvement, Center for Mental Health Services, Substance Abuse and Mental Health Services Administration.

Bebout, Richard. 2001. "Trauma-Informed Approaches." *New Directions for Mental Health Services* 89 (89): 47–55. https://doi.org/10.1002/ yd.23320018906.

Beckham, Jean C., Allison A. Roodman, Robert H. Shipley, Michael A. Hertzberg, Garry H. Cunha, Harold S. Kudler, Edward D. Levin, Jed E. Rose, and John A. Fairbank. 1995. "Smoking in Vietnam Combat Veterans with Posttraumatic Stress Disorder." *Journal of Traumatic Stress* 8 (3): 461–72. https://doi.org/10.1002/jts.2490080308.

Beike, Denise, and Erin Wirth-Beaumont. 2005. "Psychological Closure as a Memory Phenomenon." *Memory* 13 (6): 574–93. https://doi.org/ 10.1080/09658210444000241.

Beike, Denise, Laura Adams, and Erin Wirth-Beaumont. 2007. "Incomplete Inhibition of Emotion in Specific Autobiographical Memories." *Memory* 15 (4): 375–89. https://doi.org/10.1080/09658210701276850.

Benard, Bonnie. 1991. "Fostering Resilience in Children." Centre for Research on Adolescent Health and Development, August. http://crahd.phi.org/ papers/Fostering.pdf.

Bender, Kimberley, Sanna J. Thompson, Holly McManus, Janet Lantry, and Patrick M. Flynn. 2007. "Capacity for Survival: Exploring Strengths of Homeless Street Youth." *Child and Youth Care Forum* 36 (1): 25–42. https://doi.org/10.1007/s10566-006-9029-4.

Boes, Mary, and Katherine van Wormer. 1997. "Social Work with Homeless Women in Emergency Rooms: A Strengths-Feminist Perspective." *Affilia* 12 (4): 408–26. https://doi.org/10.1177/088610999701200404.

Bogar, Christine B., and Diana Hulse-Killacky. 2006. "Resilience Determinants and Resilience Processes among Female Adult Survivors of Childhood Sexual Abuse." *Journal of Counseling and Development* 84 (3): 318–27. https://doi.org/10.1002/j.1556-6678.2006.tb00411.x.

Bonanno, George A., and Dacher Keltner. 1997. "Facial Expressions of Emotion and the Course of Conjugal Bereavement." *Journal of Abnormal Psychology* 106 (1): 126–37. https://doi.org/10.1037/0021-843X.106.1.126.

Bonugli, Rebecca, Janna Lesser, and Socorro Escandon. 2013. "'The Second Thing to Hell Is Living under that Bridge': Narratives of Women Living with Victimization, Serious Mental Illness, and in Homelessness." *Issues in Mental Health Nursing* 34 (11): 827–35. https://doi.org/10.3109/01612840.2013.831149.

Boss, Pauline. 2010. "The Trauma and Complicated Grief of Ambiguous Loss." *Pastoral Psychology* 59 (2): 137–45. https://doi.org/10.1007/s11089-009-0264-0.

Bowlby, John. 1980. *Attachment and Loss.* Vol. 3: *Loss: Sadness and Depression.* New York: Basic Books.

Braun, Virginia, and Victoria Clarke. 2006. "Using Thematic Analysis in Psychology." *Qualitative Research in Psychology* 3 (2): 77–101. https://doi.org/10.1191/1478088706qp063oa.

Briere, John. 1989. *Therapy with Adults Molested as Children: Beyond Survival.* New York: Springer.

Broll, Ryan, and Laura Huey. Forthcoming. "'Every Time I Try to Get Out, I Get Pushed Back': The Role of Violent Victimization in Women's Experiences of Multiple Homelessness." *Journal of Interpersonal Violence.*

Brown, Amy L., Maria Testa, and Terri L. Messman-Moore. 2009. "Psychological Consequences of Sexual Victimization Resulting from Force, Incapacitation, or Verbal Coercion." *Violence Against Women* 15 (8): 898–919. https://doi.org/10.1177/1077801209335491.

Brown, Laura S. 2008. *Cultural Competence in Trauma Therapy: Beyond the Flashback.* Washington, DC: American Psychological Association. https://doi.org/10.1037/11752-000.

Browne, Angela. 1993. "Family Violence and Homelessness: The Relevance of Trauma Histories in the Lives of Homeless Women." *American Journal of Orthopsychiatry* 63 (3): 370–84. https://doi.org/10.1037/h0079444.

Browne, Angela, and Shari Bassuk. 1997. "Intimate Violence in the Lives of Homeless and Poor Housed Women: Prevalence and Patterns in an Ethnically Diverse Sample." *American Journal of Orthopsychiatry* 67 (2): 261–78. https://doi.org/10.1037/h0080230.

Cain, Susan. 2013. *Quiet: The Power of Introverts in a World That Can't Stop Talking.* New York: Random House.

Calvete, Esther, Susana Corral, and Ana Estevez. 2008. "Coping as a Mediator and Moderator between Intimate Partner Violence and Symptoms of

Anxiety and Depression." *Violence Against Women* 14 (8): 886–904. https://doi.org/10.1177/1077801208320907.

Canvin, Krysia, Anneli Marttila, Bo Burstrom, and Margaret Whitehead. 2009. "Tales of the Unexpected? Hidden Resilience in Poor Households in Britain." *Social Science & Medicine* 69 (2): 238–45. https://doi.org/10.1016/j.socscimed.2009.05.009.

Cappell, Howard, and Janet Greeley. 1987. "Alcohol and Tension Reduction: An Update on Research and Theory." In *Psychological Theories of Drinking and Alcoholism,* edited by H.T. Blane and K.E. Leonard, 15–54. New York: Guilford.

Centre for Addiction and Mental Health (CAMH). 2016. Trauma. http://www.camh.ca/en/hospital/health_information/a_z_mental_health_and_addiction_information/Trama/Pages/default.aspx

Child Welfare Information Gateway. 2015. *Foster Care Statistics 2013.* Washington, DC: U.S. Department of Health and Human Services, Children's Bureau. https://www.childwelfare.gov/pubPDFs/foster.pdf.

Christiansen, Dorte, Rikke Bak, and Ask Elklit. 2012. "Secondary Victims of Rape." *Violence and Victims* 27 (2): 246–62. https://doi.org/10.1891/0886-6708.27.2.246.

Cinamon, Julie S., Robert T. Muller, and Susan E. Rosenkranz. 2014. "Trauma Severity, Poly- Victimization, and Treatment Response: Adults in an Inpatient Trauma Program." *Journal of Family Violence* 29 (7): 725–37. https://doi.org/10.1007/s10896-014-9631-4.

Clements, Caroline M., and Daljit K. Sawhney. 2000. "Coping with Domestic Violence: Control Attributions, Dysphoria, and Hopelessness." *Journal of Traumatic Stress* 13 (2): 219–40. https://doi.org/10.1023/A:1007702626960.

Cohen, Marcia B. 2001. "Homeless People." In *Handbook of Social Work Practice with Vulnerable and Resilient Populations,* edited by A. Gitterman, 628–50. New York: Columbia University Press.

Collishaw, S., A. Pickles, S. Messer, M. Rutter, C. Shearer, and B. Maughan. 2007. "Resilience to Adult Psychopathology Following Childhood Maltreatment: Evidence From a Community Sample." *Child Abuse & Neglect* 31 (3): 211–29. https://doi.org/10.1016/j.chiabu.2007.02.004.

Connor, Kathryn, and Jonathan Davidson. 2003. "Development of a New Resilience Scale: The Connor Davidson Resilience Scale (CD RISC)." *Depression and Anxiety* 18 (2): 76–82. https://doi.org/10.1002/da.10113.

Connor Kathryn M., and Wei Zhang. 2006. "Resilience: Determinants, Measurement, and Treatment Responsiveness." *CNS Spectrums* 11 (S12): 5–12. https://doi.org/10.1017/S1092852900025797.

Cooke, Teri. 2015. "Understanding Women's Decision-making: The Intolerable Choice of Living in a Violent House or Escaping to the Uncertainty of Homelessness and Poverty." *Parity* 28 (4): 21–2.

Cordova, Matthew J. 2008. "Facilitating Posttraumatic Growth Following Cancer." In *Trauma, Recovery, and Growth: Positive Psychological Perspectives on Posttraumatic Stress*, edited by S. Joseph and P.A. Linley, 185–205. Hoboken, NJ: John Wiley & Sons.

Coulter, Stephen. 2014. "The Applicability of Two Strengths-based Systemic Psychotherapy Models for Young People Following Type 1 Trauma." *Child Care in Practice* 20 (1): 48–63. https://doi.org/10.1080/13575279.2013. 847057.

Creek, Jennifer, and Lesley Lougher. 2008. *Occupational Therapy in Mental Health*. 4th ed. Edinburgh: Churchill Livingstone Elsevier.

Culhane, Dennis P., and Stephen Metraux. 2008. "Rearranging the Deck Chairs or Reallocating the Lifeboats? Homelessness Assistance and Its Alternatives." *Journal of the American Planning Association* 74 (1): 111–21. https://doi.org/10.1080/01944360701821618.

Cyrulnik, Boris. 2009. *Resilience: How Your Inner Strength Can Set You Free from The Past*. New York: Penguin.

Dahlberg, Linda, and James Mercy. 2009. "History of Violence as a Public Health Issue." *AMA Virtual Mentor* 11 (2): 167–72. https://www.ncbi.nlm. nih.gov/pubmed/23190546.

Davies, Lorraine, Marilyn Ford-Gilboe, and Joanne Hammerton. 2009. "Gender Inequality and Patterns of Abuse Post-Leaving." *Journal of Family Violence* 24 (1): 27–39. https://doi.org/10.1007/s10896-008-9204-5.

Davies-Netzley, Sally, Michael Hurlburt, and Richard Hough. 1996. "Childhood Abuse as a Precursor to Homelessness for Homeless Women with Severe Mental Illness." *Violence and Victims* 11 (2): 129–42.

Deck, Stacey, and Phyllis Platt. 2015. "Homelessness Is Traumatic: Abuse, Victimization, and Trauma Histories of Homeless Men." *Journal of Aggression, Maltreatment & Trauma* 24 (9): 1022–43. https://doi.org/10.1080/ 10926771.2015.1074134.

D'Ercole, Ann, and Elmer Struening. 1990. "Victimization among Homeless Women: Implications for Service Delivery." *Journal of Community Psychology* 18 (2): 141–52. https://doi.org/10.1002/1520-6629(199004)18:2<141::AID-JCOP2290180206>3.0.CO;2-O.

Diaz, A.B., and Robert Motta. 2008. "The Effects of an Aerobic Exercise Program on Posttraumatic Stress Disorder Symptom Severity in Adolescents." *International Journal of Emergency Mental Health* 10 (1): 49–59.

Dietz, Christine. 2000. "Responding to Oppression and Abuse: A Feminist Challenge to Clinical Social Work." *Affilia* 15 (3): 369–89. https://doi.org/10.1177/08861090022094001.

Donovan, Roxanne A., and Lindsey A. West. 2015. "Stress and Mental Health: Moderating Role of the Strong Black Woman Stereotype." *Journal of Black Psychology* 41 (4): 384–96. https://doi.org/10.1177/0095798414543014.

Eckstein, Jessica J. 2011. "Reasons for Staying in Intimately Violent Relationships: Comparisons of Men and Women and Messages Communicated to Self and Others." *Journal of Family Violence* 26 (1): 21–30. https://doi.org/10.1007/s10896-010-9338-0.

Edalati, Hanie, Michael Krausz, and Christian Schutz. 2016. "Childhood Maltreatment and Revictimization in a Homeless Population." *Journal of Interpersonal Violence* 31 (14): 2492–512. https://doi.org/10.1177/0886260515576972.

Ellen, Ingrid Gould, and Brendan O'Flaherty, eds. 2010. *How to House the Homeless*. New York: Sage.

Elliott, Ann N., and Connie N. Carnes. 2001. "Reactions of Nonoffending Parents to the Sexual Abuse of their Child: A Review of the Literature." *Child Maltreatment* 6 (4): 314–31. https://doi.org/10.1177/1077559501006004005.

Epel, Elissa S., Albert Bandura, and Philip G. Zimbardo. 1999. "Escaping Homelessness: The Influences of Self-Efficacy and Time Perspective on Coping with Homelessness." *Journal of Applied Social Psychology* 29 (3): 575–96. https://doi.org/10.1111/j.1559-1816.1999.tb01402.x.

Evans, Rhonda D., and Craig J. Forsyth. 2004. "Risk Factors, Endurance of Victimization, and Survival Strategies: The Impact of the Structural Location of Men and Women on Their Experiences within the Homeless Milieus." *Sociological Spectrum* 24 (4): 479–505. https://doi.org/10.1080/02732170390260413.

Everly, George S., Jr., Dennis K. McCormack, and Douglas A. Strouse. 2012. "Seven Characteristics of Highly Resilient People: Insights from Navy SEALs to the 'Greatest Generation.'" *International Journal of Emergency Mental Health* 14: 87–93.

Federal Bureau of Investigation (FBI). 2016. "Crime in the United States, 2015." *Uniform Crime Reports.* https://ucr.fbi.gov/crime-in-the-u.s/2015/crime-in-the-u.s.-2015/offenses-known-to-law-enforcement/violent-crime/violentcrimemain_final.pdf.

Feeny, Norah C., and Lori A. Zoellner. 2014. "Conclusion: Risk and Resilience Following Trauma." In *Facilitating Resilience and Recovery Following Trauma*, edited by L.A. Zoellner and N.C. Feeny, 325–34. New York: Guilford Press.

Ferguson, Kristin, Kimberly Bender, and Sanna Thompson. 2015. "Gender, Coping Strategies, Homelessness Stressors, and Income Generation among Homeless Young Adults in Three Cities." *Social Science & Medicine* 135: 47–55. https://doi.org/10.1016/j.socscimed.2015.04.028.

Fidler, Gail S., and Jay W. Fidler. 1963. *Occupational Therapy: A Communication Process in Psychiatry.* New York: Mc Millan.

Finfgeld-Connett, Deborah. 2010. "Becoming Homeless, Being Homeless, and Resolving Homelessness among Women." *Issues in Mental Health Nursing* 31 (7): 461–9. https://doi.org/10.3109/01612840903586404.

Flemke, Kimberly. 2009. "Triggering Rage: Unresolved Trauma in Women's Lives." *Contemporary Family Therapy* 31 (2): 123–39. https://doi.org/10.1007/s10591-009-9084-8.

Fowler, Patrick J., Carolyn J. Tompsett, Jordan M. Braciszewski, Angela Jacques-Tiura, and Boris B. Baltes. 2009. "Community Violence: A Meta-analysis on the Effect of Exposure and Mental Health Outcomes of Children and Adolescents." *Development and Psychopathology* 21 (01): 227–59. https://doi.org/10.1017/S0954579409000145.

Francis, Martha E., and James W. Pennebaker. 1992. "Putting Stress into Words: The Impact of Writing on Physiological, Absentee, and Self-reported Emotional Well-being Measures." *American Journal of Health Promotion* 6 (4): 280–7. https://doi.org/10.4278/0890-1171-6.4.280.

Frazier, Patricia A., and Jeffery W. Burnett. 1994. "Immediate Coping Strategies among Rape Victims." *Journal of Counseling and Development* 72 (6): 633–9. https://doi.org/10.1002/j.1556-6676.1994.tb01694.x.

Froyum, Clarissa M. 2013. "Leaving the Street Alone: Contesting Street Manhood as a Gender Project." *Journal of Gender Studies* 22 (1): 38–53. https://doi.org/10.1080/09589236.2012.681188.

Gelberg, Lillian, C.H. Browner, Elena Lejano, and Lisa Arangua. 2004. "Access to Women's Health Care: A Qualitative Study of Barriers Perceived by Homeless Women." *Women & Health* 40 (2): 87–100. https://doi.org/10.1300/J013v40n02_06.

Gilligan, R. 2000. "Adversity, Resilience and Young People: The Protective Value of Positive School and Spare Time Experiences." *Children & Society* 14 (1): 37–47. https://doi.org/10.1111/j.1099-0860.2000.tb00149.x.

Goering, Scott Veldhuizen, Aimee Watson, Carol Adair, Brianna Kopp, Eric Latimer, Geoff Nelson, Eric MacNaughton, David Streiner, and Tim Aubry. 2014. *National at Home/Chez Soi Final Report.* Calgary, AB: Mental Health Commission of Canada.

Goldner, Jonathan, Tracy L. Peters, Maryse H. Richards, and Steven Pearce. 2011. "Exposure to Community Violence and Protective and Risky Contexts among Low-Income Urban African-American Adolescents: A Prospective Study." *Journal of Youth and Adolescence* 40 (2): 174–86. https://doi.org/10.1007/s10964-010-9527-4.

Goodman, Lisa A., and Mary Ann Dutton. 1996. "The Relationship between Victimization and Cognitive Schemata among Episodically Homeless, Seriously Mentally Ill Women." *Violence and Victims* 11: 159–74.

Goodman, Lisa A., Marry Ann Dutton, and Maxine Harris. 1997. "The Relationship between Violence Dimensions and Symptom Severity among Homeless, Mentally Ill Women." *Journal of Traumatic Stress* 10 (1): 51–70. https://doi.org/10.1002/jts.2490100106.

Goodman, Lisa A., Stanley D. Rosenberg, Kim T. Mueser, and Robert E. Drake. 1997. "Physical and Sexual Assault History in Women with Serious Mental Illness: Prevalence, Correlates, Treatment, and Future Research Directions." *Schizophrenia Bulletin* 23 (4): 685–96. https://doi.org/10.1093/schbul/23.4.685.

Goodman-Brown, Tina B., Robin S. Edelstein, Gail S. Goodman, David P.H. Jones, and David S. Gordon. 2003. "Why Children Tell: A Model of Children's Disclosure of Sexual Abuse." *Child Abuse & Neglect* 27 (5): 525–40. https://doi.org/10.1016/S0145-2134(03)00037-1.

Green, Harold D., Jr., Joan S. Tucker, Suzanne L. Wenzel, Daniela Golinelli, David P. Kennedy, Gery W. Ryan, and Annie J. Zhou. 2012. "Association of Childhood Abuse with Homeless Women's Social Networks." *Child Abuse & Neglect* 36 (1): 21–31. https://doi.org/10.1016/j.chiabu.2011.07.005.

Hamilton, Alison, Ines Poza, and Donna Washington. 2011. "'Homelessness and Trauma Go Hand-in-Hand': Pathways to Homelessness among Women Veterans." *Women's Health Issues* 21 (4 Supp): S203–9. https://doi.org/10.1016/j.whi.2011.04.005.

Halton, Dianne C. 1997. "Managing Health Problems among Homeless Women with Children in a Transitional Shelter." *Journal of Nursing Scholarship* 29 (1): 33–7. https://doi.org/10.1111/j.1547-5069.1997.tb01137.x.

Harley, Dana, and Vanessa Hunn. 2015. "Utilization of Photovoice to Explore Hope and Spirituality among Low-Income African American Adolescents." *Child & Adolescent Social Work Journal* 32 (1): 3–15. https://doi.org/10.1007/s10560-014-0354-4.

Harris, Maxine, and Roger D. Fallot, eds. 2001. *Using Trauma Theory to Design Service Systems*. San Francisco: Jossey-Bass.

Harvey, R. 2012. "Young People, Sexual Orientation, and Resilience." In *The Social Ecology of Resilience: A Handbook of Theory and Practice*, edited by M. Ungar, 325–35. New York: Springer. https://doi.org/10.1007/978-1-4614-0586-3_25.

Herman, Judith Lewis. 1992. *Trauma and Recovery: The Aftermath of Violence.* New York: Basic Books.

Heslin, Kevin C., Ronald M. Andersen, and Lillian Gelberg. 2003. "Case Management and Access to Services for Homeless Women." *Journal of Health Care for the Poor and Underserved* 14 (1): 34–51. https://doi.org/10.1353/hpu.2010.0825.

Hine, Jean, and Joanna Welford. 2012. "Girls' Violence: Criminality or Resilience?" In *The Social Ecology of Resilience: A Handbook of Theory and Practice*, edited by M. Ungar, 157–69. New York: Springer. https://doi.org/10.1007/978-1-4614-0586-3_14.

Holt, Richard L., Sylvia Montesinos, and Richard C. Christensen. 2007. "Physical and Sexual Abuse History in Women Seeking Treatment at a Psychiatric Clinic for the Homeless." *Journal of Psychiatric Practice* 13 (1): 58–60. https://doi.org/10.1097/00131746-200701000-00010.

Holt, Stephanie, Helen Buckley, and Sadhbh Whelan. 2008. "The Impact of Exposure to Domestic Violence on Children and Young People: A Review of the Literature." *Child Abuse & Neglect* 32 (8): 797–810. https://doi.org/10.1016/j.chiabu.2008.02.004.

Hopper, Elizabeth K., Ellen L. Bassuk, and Jefrrey Olivet. 2010. "Shelter from the Storm: Trauma-Informed Care in Homelessness Service Settings." *Open Health Services and Policy Journal* 3 (2): 80–100. https://doi.org/10.2174/1874924001003020080.

Hudson, Angela L., Kynna Wright, Debika Bhattacharya, Karabi Sinha, Adeline Nyamathi, and Mary Marfisee. 2010. "Correlates of Adult Assault among Homeless Women." *Journal of Health Care for the Poor and Underserved* 21: 1250–62.

Huey, Laura. 2012. *Invisible Victims: Homelessness and the Growing Security Gap.* Toronto: University of Toronto Press. https://doi.org/10.3138/9781442695788.

Huey, Laura. 2016. "There Is No Strength in Emotions: The Role of Street Enculturation in Influencing How Victimized Homeless Women Speak about Violence." *Journal of Interpersonal Violence* 31 (10): 1817–41. https://doi.org/10.1177/0886260515570749.

Huey, Laura, and Marianne Quirouette. 2010. "'Any Girl Can Call the Cops, No Problem': The Influence of Gender on Support for the Decision to Report Criminal Victimization within Homeless Communities." *British Journal of Criminology* 50 (2): 278–95. https://doi.org/10.1093/bjc/azp078.

Huey, Laura, Georgios Fthenos, and Danielle Hryniewicz. 2012. "'I Need Help and I Know I Need Help. Why Won't Nobody Listen to Me?' Trauma and Homeless Women's Experiences with Accessing and Consuming Mental

Health Services." *Society and Mental Health* 2 (2): 120–34. https://doi.org/10.1177/2156869312445287.

Huey, Laura, Ryan Broll, Danielle Hyrniewicz, and Georgios Fthenos. 2014. "'They Just Asked Me Why I Became Homeless': 'Failure to Ask' as a Barrier to Homeless Women's Ability to Access Services Post-Victimization." *Violence and Victims* 29 (6): 952–66. https://doi.org/10.1891/0886-6708.VV-D-12-00121.

Huey, Laura, and Rose Ricciardelli. 2016. *Adding Insult to Injury: (Mis)Treating Homeless Women in Our Mental Health System.* Boulder, CO: Lynne Reinner Publishers.

Hyde, Justeen. 2005. "From Home to Street: Understanding Young People's Transitions into Homelessness." *Journal of Adolescence* 28 (2): 171–83. https://doi.org/10.1016/j.adolescence.2005.02.001.

Iveson, Mandie, and Flora Cornish. 2016. "Re-building Bridges: Homeless People's Views on the Role of Vocational and Educational Activities in Their Everyday Lives." *Journal of Community & Applied Social Psychology* 26 (3): 253–67. https://doi.org/10.1002/casp.2262.

Jaffee, Sara R., Avshalom Caspi, Terrie B. Moffitt, Monica Polo-Tomás, and Alan Taylor. 2007. "Individual, Family, and Neighborhood Factors Distinguish Resilient from Non-Resilient Children: A Cumulative Stressors Model." *Child Abuse & Neglect* 31 (3): 231–53. https://doi.org/10.1016/j.chiabu.2006.03.011.

Janoff-Bulman, Ronnie. 1992. *Shattered Assumptions: Towards a New Psychology of Trauma.* New York: Free Press.

Jasinski, Jana. L., Jennifer K. Wesely, James D. Wright, and Elizabeth E. Mustaine. 2010. *Hard Lives, Mean Streets: Violence in the Lives of Homeless Women.* Lebanon, ME: Northeastern University Press.

Jones, Elsa. 2007. *Working with Adult Survivors of Child Sexual Abuse.* London: Karnac Books.

Joseph, Stephen. 2011. *What Doesn't Kill Us: The New Psychology of Posttraumatic Growth.* New York: Basic Books.

Karabanow, J., and S. Kidd. 2014. "Being Young and Homeless: Addressing Youth Homelessness from Drop-in to Drafting Policy." In *Homelessness and Health in Canada*, edited by M. Guirguis-Younger, R. McNeil, and S. Hwang, 13–34. Ottawa: University of Ottawa Press.

Keltner, Dacher, and George A. Bonanno. 1997. "A Study of Laughter and Dissociation: Distinct Correlates of Laughter and Smiling During Bereavement." *Journal of Personality and Social Psychology* 73 (4): 687–702. https://doi.org/10.1037/0022-3514.73.4.687.

Kidd, Sean A., and Larry Davidson. 2007. "'You Have to Adapt Because You Have No Other Choice': The Stories of Strength and Resilience of 208

Homeless Youth in New York City and Toronto." *Journal of Community Psychology* 35 (2): 219–38. https://doi.org/10.1002/jcop.20144.

Kidd, Sean A., Tyler Frederick, Jeff Karabanow, Jean Hughes, Ted Naylor, and Skye Barbic. 2016. "A Mixed Methods Study of Recently Homeless Youth Efforts to Sustain Housing and Stability." *Child & Adolescent Social Work Journal* 33 (3): 207–18.

Kilpatrick, Dean G., Ron Acierno, Heidi S. Resuick, Benjamin E. Saunders, and Connie L. Best. 1997. "A 2-Year Longitudinal Analysis of the Relationship between Violence Assault and Substance Use in Women." *Journal of Consulting and Clinical Psychology* 65 (5): 834–47. https://doi.org/10.1037/0022-006X.65.5.834.

Klitzing, Sandra Wolf. 2004. "Women Living in a Homeless Shelter: Stress, Coping and Leisure." *Journal of Leisure Research* 36 (4): 483–512.

Kurtz, Steven, Hilary Surratt, James Inciardi, and Marion Kiley. 2004. "Sex Work and 'Date' Violence." *Violence Against Women* 10 (4): 357–85. https://doi.org/10.1177/1077801204263199.

Lam, Julie A., and Robert Rosenheck. 1998. "The Effect of Victimization on Clinical Outcomes of Homeless Persons with Serious Mental Illness." *Psychiatric Services* 49 (5): 678–83. https://doi.org/10.1176/ps.49.5.678.

Larney, Sarah, Elizabeth Conroy, Katherine L. Mills, Lucy Burns, and Maree Teesson. 2009. "Factors Associated with Violent Victimisation among Homeless Adults in Sydney, Australia." *Australian and New Zealand Journal of Public Health* 33 (4): 347–51. https://www.ncbi.nlm.nih.gov/pubmed/19689595.

Lepore, Stephen J., and Melanie A. Greenberg. 2002. "Mending Broken Hearts: Effects of Expressive Writing on Mood, Cognitive, Processing, Social Adjustment, and Health Following a Relationship Breakup." *Psychology & Health* 17 (5): 547–60. https://doi.org/10.1080/08870440290025768.

Lewinson, Terri, M. Lori Thomas, and Shaneureka White. 2014. "Traumatic Transitions: Homeless Women's Narratives of Abuse, Loss, and Fear." *Affilia* 29 (2): 192–205. https://doi.org/10.1177/0886109913516449.

London, Kamala, Maggie Bruck, Stephen J. Ceci, and Daniel W. Shuman. 2005. "Disclosure of Child Sexual Abuse: What Does the Research Tell Us about the Ways That Children Tell?" *Psychology, Public Policy, and Law* 11 (1): 194–226. https://doi.org/10.1037/1076-8971.11.1.194.

Mackenzie-Mohr, Suzanne, John Coates, and Heather McLeod. 2012. "Responding to the Needs of Youth Who Are Homeless: Calling for Politicized Trauma-Informed Intervention." *Children and Youth Services Review* 34 (1): 136–43. https://doi.org/10.1016/j.childyouth.2011.09.008.

Maggio, Mark J. 2006. "Hurricane Katrina: Resilience, the Other Side of Tragedy." *Federal Probation* 70: 42–4.

Masten, Ann S. 2011. "Resilience in Children Threatened by Extreme Adversity: Frameworks for Research, Practice, and Translational Synergy." *Development and Psychopathology* 23 (02): 493–506. https://doi.org/10.1017/S0954579411000198.

Masten, Ann, K.M. Best, and N. Garmezy. 1990. "Resilience and Development: Contributions from the Study of Children Who Overcome Adversity." *Development and Psychopathology* 2 (4): 425–44. https://doi.org/10.1017/S0954579400005812.

Masten, Ann S., J.J. Cutulli, Janette E. Herbers, Elizabeth Hinz, Jelena Obradović, and Amanda J. Wenzel. 2014. "Academic Risk and Resilience in the Context of Homelessness." *Child Development Perspectives* 8 (4): 201–6. https://doi.org/10.1111/cdep.12088.

Maté, Gabor. 2008. *In the Realm of Hungry Ghosts: Close Encounters with Addiction*. Toronto: Vintage Canada.

McClendon, Jennifer, and Shannon Lane. 2014. "Homeless People." In *Handbook of Social Work Practice with Vulnerable and Resilient Populations*, 3rd ed., edited by A. Gitterman, 345–65. New York: Columbia University Press. https://doi.org/10.7312/gitt11396-018.

McManus, Holly, and Sanna J. Thompson. 2008. "Trauma among Unaccompanied Homeless Youth: The Integration of Street Culture into a Model of Intervention." *Journal of Aggression, Maltreatment & Trauma* 16 (1): 92–109. https://doi.org/10.1080/10926770801920818.

Meichenbaum, Donald. 2013. "Ways to Bolster Resilience Across the Deployment Cycle." In *Military Psychologists' Desk Reference*, edited by Bret Moore and Jeffrey Barnett, 325–30. Oxford: Oxford University Press. https://doi.org/10.1093/med:psych/9780199928262.003.0067.

Mikhail, Blanche I., and Mary Ann Curry. 1999. "Perceived Impediments to Prenatal Care among Low-Income Women." *Western Journal of Nursing Research* 21 (3): 335–55. https://doi.org/10.1177/019394599902100305.

Milburn, Norweeta, and Ann D'Ercole. 1991. "Homeless Women: Moving Toward a Comprehensive Model." *American Psychologist* 46 (11): 1161–19. https://doi.org/10.1037/0003-066X.46.11.1161.

Molina-Jackson, Edna. 2007. *Homeless Not Hopeless: The Survival Networks of Latino and African American Men*. New York: University Press of America.

Mullins, Christopher, and Robin Cardwell-Mullins. 2006. "Bad Ass or Punk Ass? The Contours of Street Masculinity." *Universitas* 2 (2): 1–4. https://www.researchgate.net/publication/254910253_Bad_Ass_or_Punk_Ass_The_Contours_of_Street_Masculinity.

Namkoong, Jae-Eun, and Andrew Gershoff. 2012. "Moving on and Away: Closure Increases Psychological Distance Through Emotion." *Advances in Consumer Research* 40: 690.

Netto, Gina, Hal Pawson, and Cathy Sharp. 2009. "Preventing Homelessness due to Domestic Violence: Providing a Safe Space or Closing the Door to New Possibilities?" *Social Policy and Administration* 43 (7): 719–35. https://doi.org/10.1111/j.1467-9515.2009.00691.x.

Norris, Fran H. 1990. "Screening for Traumatic Stress: A Scale for Use in the General Population." *Journal of Applied Social Psychology* 20 (20): 1704–15. https://doi.org/10.1111/j.1559-1816.1990.tb01505.x.

North, Carol S., and Elizabeth M. Smith. 1992. "Posttraumatic Stress Disorder among Homeless Men and Women." *Hospital & Community Psychiatry* 43: 1010–16.

Padgett, Deborah K., Leyla Gulcur, and Sam Tsemberis. 2006. "Housing First Services for People who are Homeless with Co-Occurring Serious Mental Illness and Substance Abuse." *Research on Social Work Practice* 16 (1): 74–83. https://doi.org/10.1177/1049731505282593.

Padgett, Deborah K., Ben Henwood, Courtney Abrams, and Robert E. Drake. 2008. "Social Relationships Among Persons Who Have Experienced Serious Mental Illness, Substance Abuse, and Homelessness: Implications for Recovery." *American Journal of Orthopsychiatry* 78 (3): 333–9. https://doi.org/10.1037/a0014155.

Park, Crystal L., and Slattery, Jeanne M. 2014. "Resilience Interventions with a Focus on Meanings and Values." In *The Resilience Handbook: Approaches to Stress and Trauma*, edited by M. Kent, M.C. Davis, and J.W. Reich, 370–82. New York: Routledge.

Patterson, Allisha, and Roger Tweed. 2009. "Escaping Homelessness: Anticipated and Perceived Facilitators." *Journal of Community Psychology* 37 (7): 846–58. https://doi.org/10.1002/jcop.20335.

Perron, Brian E., Ben Alexander-Eitzman, David F. Gillespie, and David Pollio. 2008. "Modeling the Mental Health Effects of Victimization among Homeless Persons." *Social Science & Medicine* 67 (9): 1475–9. https://doi.org/10.1016/j.socscimed.2008.07.012.

Perron, Jeff, Kristin Cleverley, and Sean Kidd. 2014. "Resilience, Loneliness, and Psychological Distress Among Homeless Youth." *Archives of Psychiatric Nursing* 28 (4): 226–9. https://doi.org/10.1016/j.apnu.2014.05.004.

Richmond, Therese S., Hilaire J. Thompson, Janet A. Deatrick, and Donald R. Kauder. 2000. "Journey towards Recovery Following Physical Trauma." *Journal of Advanced Nursing* 32 (6): 1341–7. https://doi.org/10.1046/j.1365-2648.2000.01629.x.

Rutter, Michael. 1987. "Psychosocial Resilience and Protective Mechanisms." *American Journal of Orthopsychiatry* 57 (3): 316–31. https://doi.org/10.1111/j.1939-0025.1987.tb03541.x.

Salomon, Amy, Shari S. Bassuk, and Nicholas Huntington. 2002. "The Relationship between Intimate Partner Violence and the Use of Addictive Substances in Poor and Homeless Mothers." *Violence Against Women* 8 (7): 785–815. https://doi.org/10.1177/107780102400388489.

Sanders, Jackie, Robyn Munford, and Linda Liebenberg. 2012. "Young People, Their Families and Social Supports: Understanding Resilience with Complexity Theory." In *The Social Ecology of Resilience: A Handbook of Theory and Practice*, edited by M. Ungar, 233–43. New York: Springer. https://doi.org/10.1007/978-1-4614-0586-3_19.

Seiffge-Krenke, Inge. 2004. "Adaptive and Maladaptive Coping Styles: Does Intervention Change Anything." In *Social Cognition in Adolescence*, edited by Willem Koops and Harke Bosma, 367–82. New York: Taylor and Francis. https://doi.org/10.1080/17405629.2004.11453396.

Shannon, Kate, Thomas Kerr, Stephanie A. Strathdee, Jean Shoveller, Julio S. Montaner, and Mark W. Tyndall. 2009. "Prevalence and Structural Correlates of Gender Based Violence among a Prospective Cohort of Female Sex Workers." *British Medical Journal* 339: 1–8.

Shinn, Marybeth. 2010. "Homelessness, Poverty, and Social Exclusion in the United States and Europe." *European Journal of Homelessness* 4: 19–44.

Smith, Bruce, J. Alexis Ortiz, Kathryn Wiggins, Jennifer Bernard, and Jeanne Dalen. 2011. "Spirituality, Emotions and Positive Emotions." In *The Oxford Handbook of Psychology and Spirituality*, edited by Lisa J. Miller, 455–67. Oxford: Oxford University Press.

Stein, Bradley D., Lisa H. Jaycox, Sheryl Kataoka, Hilary J. Rhodes, and Katherine D. Vestal. 2003. "Prevalence of Child and Adolescent Exposure to Community Violence." *Clinical and Family Psychology Review* 6 (4): 247–64. https://doi.org/10.1023/B:CCFP.0000006292.61072.d2.

Stenius, Vanja, and Bonita Veysey. 2005. "'It's the Little Things': Women, Trauma, and Strategies for Healing." *Journal of Interpersonal Violence* 20 (10): 1155–74. https://doi.org/10.1177/0886260505278533.

Stermac, Lana, and Emily K. Paradis. 2001. "Homeless Women and Victimization: Abuse and Mental Health History among Homeless Rape Survivors." *Resources for Feminist Research* 28: 65–80.

Stump, Monica J., and Jane Ellen Smith. 2008. "The Relationship between Posttraumatic Growth and Substance Use in Homeless Women with Histories of Traumatic Experience." *American Journal on Addictions* 17 (6): 478–87. https://doi.org/10.1080/10550490802409017.

Taylor, Shelley E., Margaret E. Kemeny, Geoffrey M. Reed, Julienne E. Bower, and Tara Gruenewald. 2000. "Psychological Resources, Positive

Illusions, and Health." *American Psychologist* 55 (1): 99–109. https://doi.org/10.1037/0003-066X.55.1.99.

Thomas, Denis A., and Marianne Woodside. 2011. "Resilience in Adult Children of Divorce: A Multiple Case Study." *Marriage & Family Review* 47 (4): 213–34. https://doi.org/10.1080/01494929.2011.586300.

Thomas, Yvonne, Marion Gray, Sue McGinty, and Sally Ebringer. 2011. "Homeless Adults' Engagement in Art: First Steps Towards Identity, Recovery and Social Inclusion." *Australian Occupational Therapy* 58 (6): 429–36. https://doi.org/10.1111/j.1440-1630.2011.00977.x.

Thompson, Sanna J., Holly McManus, and Tanya Voss. 2006. "Posttraumatic Stress Disorder and Substance Abuse among Youth Who Are Homeless: Treatment Issues and Implications." *Brief Treatment and Crisis Intervention* 6 (3): 206–17. https://doi.org/10.1093/brief-treatment/mhl002.

Thompson, Sanna J., Tiffany N. Ryan, Katherine L. Montgomery, Angie Del Prado Lippman, Kimberly Bender, and Kristin Ferguson. 2013. "Perceptions of Resilience and Coping: Homeless Young Adults Speak Out." *Youth & Society* 48 (1): 58–76. https://doi.org/10.1177/0044118X13477427.

Tischler, Victoria, Alison Rademeyer, and Panos Vostanis. 2007. "Mothers Experiencing Homelessness: Mental Health, Support and Social Care Needs." *Health & Social Care in the Community* 15 (3): 246–53. https://doi.org/10.1111/j.1365-2524.2006.00678.x.

Tsai, Alexander, Sheri Weiser, Samantha Dilworth, Martha Shumway, and Elise Riley. 2015. "Violent Victimization, Mental Health, and Service Utilization Outcomes in a Cohort of Homeless and Unstably Housed Women Living with or at Risk of Becoming Infected With HIV." *American Journal of Epidemiology* 181 (10): 817–26. https://doi.org/10.1093/aje/kwu350.

Tsemberis, Sam, Leyla Gulcur, and Maria Nakae. 2004. "Housing First, Consumer Choice, and Harm Reduction for Homeless Individuals with a Dual Diagnosis." *American Journal of Public Health* 94 (4): 651–6. https://doi.org/10.2105/AJPH.94.4.651.

Tusaie, Kathleen, and Janice Dyer. 2004. "Resilience: A Historical Review of the Construct." *Holistic Nursing Practice* 18 (1): 3–8, quiz 9–10. https://doi.org/10.1097/00004650-200401000-00002.

Tutty, Leslie M., Cindy Ogden, Bianca Giurgiu, and Gillian Weaver-Dunlop. 2013. "I Built My House of Hope: Abused Women and Pathways into Homelessness." *Violence Against Women* 19 (12): 1498–517. https://doi.org/10.1177/1077801213517514.

Ullman, Sarah E. 1996. "Social Reactions, Coping Strategies, and Self-Blame Attributions in Adjustment to Sexual Assault." *Psychology of Women*

Quarterly 20 (4): 505–26. https://doi.org/10.1111/j.1471-6402.1996.tb00319.x.

Ungar, M. 2004. *Nurturing Hidden Resilience in Troubled Youth*. Toronto: University of Toronto Press.

Ungar, M. 2005. "Delinquent or Simply Resilient? How 'Problem' Behaviour Can Be a Child's Hidden Path to Resilience" (August). *Voices for Children*. Retrieved from http://www.resilienceproject.org/files/PDF/Delinquent%20or%20simple%20resilient.pdf.

Ungar, M. 2006. "Nurturing Hidden Resilience in At-Risk Youth in Different Cultures." *Journal of the Canadian Academy of Child and Adolescent Psychiatry* 15 (2): 53–8.

Upshur, Carole C., Linda Weinreb, and Monica Bharel. 2014. "Homeless Women and Hazardous Drinking: Screening Results in a Primary Health Care Setting." *American Journal on Addictions* 23 (2): 117–22. https://doi.org/10.1111/j.1521-0391.2013.12072.x.

Valentine, Lanae, and Leslie L. Feinauer. 1993. "Resilience Factors Associated with Female Survivors of Childhood Sexual Abuse." *American Journal of Family Therapy* 21 (3): 216–24. https://doi.org/10.1080/01926189308250920.

Valerio, Paola, and Georgia Lepper. 2009. "Sorrow, Shame, and Self-Esteem: Perception of Self and Others in Groups for Women Survivors of Child Sexual Abuse." *Psychoanalytic Psychotherapy* 23 (2): 136–53. https://doi.org/10.1080/02668730902920405.

Vidal, Maria E., and Jenny Petrak. 2007. "Shame and Adult Sexual Assault: A Study with a Group of Female Survivors Recruited from an East London Population." *Sexual and Relationship Therapy* 22 (2): 159–71. https://doi.org/10.1080/14681990600784143.

Waaktaar, Trine, and Svenn Torgersen. 2010. "How Resilient Are Resilience Scales? The Big Five Scales Outperform Resilience Scales in Predicting Adjustment in Adolescents." *Scandinavian Journal of Psychology* 51 (2): 157–63. https://doi.org/10.1111/j.1467-9450.2009.00757.x.

Wagner, David, and Jennifer Gilman. 2012. *Confronting Homelessness: Poverty, Politics, and the Failure of Social Policy*. Denver, CO: Lynne Reinner.

Wakai, Sara, Susan Sampl, Laura Hilton, and Beyonka Ligon. 2014. "Women in Prison: Self-Injurious Behavior, Risk Factors, Psychological Function, and Gender-Specific Interventions." *The Prison Journal* 94 (3): 347–64. https://doi.org/10.1177/0032885514537602.

Wardhaugh, Julia. 1999. "The Unaccommodated Woman: Home, Homelessness and Identity." *Sociological Review* 47 (1): 91–109. https://doi.org/10.1111/1467-954X.00164.

Watkins, Adam M., and Terrance Taylor. 2016. "The Prevalence, Predictors and Criminogenic Effect of Joining a Gang among Urban, Suburban and Rural Youth." *Journal of Criminal Justice* 47 (1): 133–42. https://doi.org/10.1016/j.jcrimjus.2016.09.001.

Waugh, Christian E. 2014. "The Regulatory Power of Positive Emotions in Stress: A Temporal-Functional Approach." In *The Resilience Handbook: Approaches to Stress and Trauma*, edited by M. Kent, M.C. Davis, and J.W. Reich, 73–85. New York: Routledge.

Weiss, Karen G. 2010. "Too Ashamed to Report: Deconstructing the Shame of Sexual Victimization." *Feminist Criminology* 5 (3): 286–310. https://doi.org/10.1177/1557085110376343.

Wenzel, Suzanne L., Paul Koegel, and Lillian Gelberg. 2000. "Antecedents of Physical and Sexual Victimization among Homeless Women: A Comparison to Homeless Men." *American Journal of Community Psychology* 28 (3): 367–90. https://doi.org/10.1023/A:1005157405618.

Wenzel, Suzanne L., Barbara D. Leake, and Lillian Gelberg. 2001. "Risk Factors for Major Violence among Homeless Women." *Journal of Interpersonal Violence* 16 (8): 739–52. https://doi.org/10.1177/088626001016008001.

Wenzel, Suzanne L., Ronald M. Andersen, Deidre Spelliscy Gifford, and Lillian Gelberg. 2001. "Homeless Women's Gynecological Symptoms and Use of Medical Care." *Journal of Health Care for the Poor and Underserved* 12 (3): 323–41. https://doi.org/10.1353/hpu.2010.0797.

Werner, Emmy E., and Ruth S. Smith. 2001. *Journeys from Childhood to Midlife: Risk, Resilience, and Recovery.* Ithaca, NY: Cornell University Press.

Wesely, Jennifer K., and James D. Wright. 2009. "From the Inside Out: Efforts by Homeless Women to Disrupt Cycles of Crime and Violence." *Women & Criminal Justice* 19 (3): 217–34. https://doi.org/10.1080/08974450903001552.

Whitbeck, Les B. 2009. *Mental Health and Emerging Adulthood among Homeless Young People.* New York: Taylor and Francis.

Whitbeck, Les B., Brian E. Armenta, and Kari C. Gentzler. 2015. "Homelessness-Related Traumatic Events and PTSD Among Women Experiencing Episodes of Homelessness in Three U.S. Cities." *Journal of Trauma Stress* 28 (4): 355–60.

Williams, Jean Calterone. 2016. *A Roof Over My Head: Homeless Women and the Shelter Industry.* Boulder: University Press of Colorado.

Williams, Nancy R., and Elizabeth W. Lindsey. 2005. "Spirituality and Religion in the Lives of Runaway and Homeless Youth: Coping with Adversity." *Journal of Religion and Spirituality in Social Work: Social Thought* 24: 19–38.

Williams, Nancy R., Elizabeth W. Lindsey, P. David Kurtz, and Sara Jarvis. 2001. "From Trauma to Resiliency: Lessons from Former Runaway and Homeless Youth." *Journal of Youth Studies* 4(2): 233–53.

Wilson, Joshua M., Jenny E. Fauci, and Lisa A. Goodman. 2015. "Bringing Trauma-Informed Practice to Domestic Violence Programs: A Qualitative Analysis of Current Approaches." *American Journal of Orthopsychiatry* 85 (6): 586–99. https://doi.org/10.1037/ort0000098.

Wolak, Janis, and David Finkelhor. 1998. "Children Exposed to Partner Violence." In *Partner Violence: A Comprehensive Review of 20 Years of Research*, edited by J.L. Jasinski and L.M. Williams, 73–112. Thousand Oaks, CA: Sage.

Yoder, Kevin, Les Whitbeck, and Dan Hoyt. 2001. "Event History Analysis of Antecedents to Running Away from Home and Being on the Street." *American Behavioral Scientist* 45 (1): 51–65. https://doi.org/10.1177/00027640121957015.

Index

Salomon, A., 24, 60
Salvation Army, 20
Samantha, 98
Sanders, J., 29
Sandra, 84
scales
 psychological, 30
 standardized, 30
scars, 33, 36, 51–2, 71
Schutz, C., 36
secrets, carrying, 88
security, 6, 77, 85, 87, 105
 income, 109
 ontological, 108
Seiffge-Krenke, I., 9
self, 6, 28, 53, 55, 65
 spiritual, 92
self-acceptance, 73
self-appraisals, critical, 56
self-blame, 51, 53–4, 66
self-care tasks, 57
self-confidence, 80–1, 84
self-defeating, 99
self-defence, 42
self-descriptions, 16
self-doubt, 62, 109
self-efficacy, 8
self-esteem, 80, 83, 85, 91, 94, 102,
 112–14
 issues of, 56, 84, 93
self-expression, 102, 113
 creative, 13
self-medication, 60
self-protection, 9
serious mental illness (SMI), 77
services, 10–11, 18, 28, 62, 67, 92–3,
 112, 115–16
 access to psychiatric, 115
 current systems of, 115
 healthcare, 10, 62, 67

post-victimization, 10
 psychological, 28
 therapeutic, 68, 114–15
service workers, 28, 115
setbacks, 7, 66
 significant, 74, 109
sex, 15, 38, 42–4
 consensual, 43
 trading, 43
sex workers, 43
sexual abuse, 4, 25, 31, 36, 39–40,
 53–4, 61, 66, 69, 88–90, 96
sexual assaults, 15, 25, 27, 30–1, 33,
 42–3, 56, 58, 66–7, 69, 90, 96, 98, 109
sexual exploitation, 85
sexual identity, 29
sexualization, early, 56
shame, 12, 33, 51, 53, 55–6, 62, 66,
 73, 88
 carrying, 33
 feelings of, 53, 109
shame-based self-narratives, 53
Shania, 75
Shannon, K., 43
Sharleen, 17, 24, 45–6, 59, 71, 102
shelters, 10–11, 18–22, 24–5, 27–8,
 43–4, 47, 61, 66–7, 70–1, 75–6,
 84, 88, 91, 93, 101–4
 workers in, 57
Sheran, 24, 37–8, 44, 70
shooting, 15, 46, 48, 60
significant violence, 16
 observed, 25–6
 witnessed, 25, 45–6
Simone, 22
Sindy, 88
Skid Row, Los Angeles, 46–7
"Skid Row Sister," 102
skills, 13, 82–3, 101
 communication, 94

Lightning Source UK Ltd.
Milton Keynes UK
UKHW010000271021
392512UK00010B/366

9 781442 626850